The
Little
Black
Dress

The Little Black Dress

Tracy Martin

Illustrations by Lord Dunsby

How to dress perfectly for any occasion

CICO BOOKS

LONDON   NEW YORK

Published in 2012 by CICO Books
An imprint of Ryland Peters & Small Ltd

20–21 Jockey's Fields   519 Broadway, 5th Floor
London WC1R 4BW   New York, NY 10012

www.cicobooks.com

10 9 8 7 6 5 4 3 2 1

A CIP catalog record for this book is available from the
Library of Congress and the British Library.

ISBN: 978-1-908862-02-0

Printed in China

Editor: Ingrid Court-Jones

Designer: Louise Leffler

Illustrator: Lord Dunsby (aka Steve Millington,
www.lorddunsby.co.uk)

For digital editions, visit
www.cicobooks.com/apps.php

contents

Introduction

"Fashion fades, style is eternal."
Yves Saint Laurent, fashion designer

The perfectly dressed woman is aware of the need to look fabulous at all times. Immaculately dressed and impeccably groomed, she is confident, sophisticated, elegant, and chic. She is able to appraise a situation and then dress accordingly—classic and conservative when the need arises or with extravagance and flamboyance if the occasion demands a touch of sparkle. Conscious of both her body shape and her individual personality, she will only ever wear flattering outfits but, above all, she is a woman who recognizes you can only truly be dressed to perfection if you have a sensational sense of style.

Wallis Simpson, Marilyn Monroe, and Audrey Hepburn, along with Brigitte Bardot and Grace Kelly, are renowned for being among the most glamorous and stylish women of their time. In more recent years actress Sarah Jessica-Parker, supermodel Kate Moss, and pop star Lady Gaga also display their own very distinctive styles. Classed as leading lights in fashion, these women set the tone that the rest of us aspire to follow. So what constitutes style? Where do you begin? And how easy is it to achieve?

Much is dependant on your own style initiatives, as your personal opinions and tastes can be very different from those of the next woman. For example, some might consider Katharine Hepburn to be the most stylish woman to have walked the planet, while others disagree and prefer the outrageous fashion choices of actress Helena Bonham Carter. Style is basically in the eye of the beholder, but there are some fundamental fashion rules that even the most flamboyant dressers need to adhere to.

> *"I'm nothing to look at, so all I can do is dress better than anyone else."*
> *Wallis Simpson, Duchess of Windsor and style icon*

As with everything you first need to lay the foundations by identifying and developing your own unique style. No two women are the same, so it's important to discover the look that best suits both your personality and your figure. Owning a wardrobe of fashion staples is essential, as you need to cover every eventuality so that you can dress to impress at any important engagement. If you then merge these criteria together, you will be well on your way to becoming the epitome of style.

However, being the most stylish woman in a room isn't just about the clothing you choose to wear—there are other more crucial factors to take into consideration. Possessing elegance, class, and taste is paramount, as you cannot pull off a great look if you are unable to conduct yourself in the right way. Also, you need to ensure that your clothes and accessories complement each other and that no single item overpowers the others—unless, of course, you are making a particular fashion statement.

In fact, to become the ultimate style goddess you must consider many diverse elements when choosing your clothes, from the cut of an outfit to which design suits you best. First, you need to choose the type of fabric, along with whether to go for plain material or a pattern or print (which can be flattering or fattening.) Then you have to select the best color, which can be a dilemma as it needs to suit your skin tone and complement your mood as well as be appropriate for the event you are attending. And, of course, you also need to ensure that your personal grooming is immaculate: well-cut, tidy hair, perfectly applied make-up, and manicured nails.

> *"Elegance is a question of personality*
> *more than one's clothing."*
> *Jean-Paul Gautier, fashion designer*

Looking good at all times may initially seem complex, time-consuming, expensive, and hard work, but with the help of this book, it won't be long before you'll find dressing well becomes second nature. Crammed full of interesting tips, style guides, and facts that will help you achieve your inner style, *The Little Black Dress* advises on what to wear for every occasion, which accessories will complement your look, and what's hot and what's not in the style stakes. Textiles, shape, cut, and design are also considered and this book investigates the historic origins of classic cuts and shapes, giving an insight into how designers have gained their inspiration, and proving that fashion really does go round in circles.

A book that no style sensation should be without, it will aid you in improving your wardrobe and, in turn, enhance your lifestyle. So if you are ready to become proficient in dressing to impress, first look at the Style Checklist overleaf and then we'll start where every style-savvy woman should begin—with the most iconic design of all, the Little Black Dress (LBD) ...

Style Checklist

✹ Always buy clothes that flatter your figure and suit your personality. Never be tempted to step out of your comfort zone unless you can carry off the look with panache.

✹ Unlike most men, women seek attention through the way they look and like to be admired. Wear an outfit that makes you stand out from the crowd, but only in a positive way.

✹ Don't be swayed by current fashion fads. Just because a garment is a must-have for this season in some people's eyes, doesn't necessarily mean it's right for you.

✹ Choose quality over quantity. Invest wisely by buying the best that you can afford, especially when purchasing classic staple outfits. They will then not only look fantastic, but also stand the test of time.

✹ Consider color carefully and pick shades that enhance your skin tone, reflect your mood, and complement the occasion.

✹ Accessories add the finishing touches to any outfit, so ensure they are as striking or as understated as your look dictates.

✹ Be aware of which outfits are suitable for particular engagements. For example, arriving at a funeral in a canary yellow, lycra, low-cut mini dress would be frowned upon, even if you personally saw the occasion as a happy, celebratory event. So always give thought to where you are going and which outfit will be the most appropriate.

✹ Plan your outfit ahead of time. Try on a few combinations and show them to your friends and family before the event, so they can help you decide which one will have the most positive impact.

✻ A polished appearance is essential. Your hair, make-up, and nails all need to be preened to perfection. No matter what outfit you wear, if you haven't washed your hair for days, have plastered your make-up on in the dark, and have failed to re-paint your chipped nails, your fabulous outfit will not be the focal point. Instead, people will notice your lack of grooming.

✻ Always look after your clothes. Keep them spotless, routinely dry clean them, and hang them in the closet rather than leaving them crumpled in a drawer. If, however, any of your clothes have noticeable signs of wear and tear—yes, even your favorite dress—do not let it adorn your body again in public; instead re-cycle it by sending it to a thrift (charity) shop.

Chapter 1

The Little Black Dress (LBD)

The golden rule of fashion is that no woman's wardrobe is complete without a sophisticated yet simple Little Black Dress. A staple garment, it should have a clean silhouette and a feminine elegance, and be short in length as well as versatile enough for any occasion. A design classic, from its first appearance the LBD revolutionized the way women dressed, and even today it is considered one of the most important garments for a woman to own.

The Origins of the LBD

We have iconic French fashion designer, Gabrielle "Coco" Chanel to thank for bringing the LBD into our lives and, of course, into our wardrobes. Renowned for turning fashion completely on its head, Chanel had already liberated women from the constraints of the corset and in the early part of the twentieth century introduced more practical women's clothing in the form of boyish sportswear, suits, and unisex pants. However, it was the Little Black Dress that was to be her most groundbreaking fashion statement when it first made an appearance in 1926.

Throughout both the Victorian and Edwardian eras the color black had been reserved for those in full mourning; in fact, it was considered indecent to wear black otherwise. Chanel dismissed this prehistoric attitude to color by designing a plain, black, sleeveless, calf-length, sexy dress. An immediate success, not only did it catch the eye of women who appreciated fashion, but it also grabbed the attention of the industry as a whole.

Vogue magazine labeled the dress as "Chanel's Ford," insinuating that it was comparable to Henry Ford's Model-T car—simply designed and economically priced—and so ensuring that every woman was able to own one. It was also said that the Little Black Dress would become a sort of uniform for all women of taste, a prophecy that has surely come true.

It is easy to see why this simply cut, plain dress was so alluring. Color had reigned supreme for some time, with heavy prints, embellishments, and embroidery adorning most women's garments, especially dresses. The LBD was a complete contrast. Its sleek lines outlined a silhouette that possessed an air of restrained elegance, and so to this day, this garment has become perhaps the most vital ingredient in every woman's wardrobe.

"When the Little Black Dress is right, there is nothing else to wear in its place."

Wallis Simpson, Duchess of Windsor and style icon

The LBD Rules

You would be mistaken in believing that every short black dress automatically qualifies for the higher status of an LBD, because not all such dresses are considered chic enough. In fact, in order to qualify as an LBD, a dress must meet certain rigid criteria.

Length—The dress should be short (the very reason it's referred to as "The Little Black Dress",) so it should generally sit on or above the knee and should be no longer than calf-length. (However, as with all rules there are exceptions—see page 18.)

Cut—Simplicity is the key to this classic design, but you also need to take into consideration that the dress must be flattering. The shift is the most common shape for the LBD, as it possesses clean lines that suit the majority of body types. Women with a fuller figure may prefer to opt for a wrap dress as this will accentuate their curves. Another crucial factor is that the dress should be traditional in style rather than at the cutting-edge of fashion. Chanel once said "Fashion passes, style remains," so steer clear of trend-setting dresses that only last for one season. Your LBD is required to stand the test of time.

Fabric—LBDs come in an assortment of materials and there is no real hard and fast rule regarding which you should choose. Some say Chanel's first LBD was produced from silk and featured a slashed neckline, while others believe it was made from wool, had long sleeves for daytime, and came in other variations in a choice of satin, crêpe, or velvet for the evening. So the choice of fabric is really up to the individual, although it's important always to select a material that is flattering to the figure. Silk and satin are both excellent choices as they work well for all sizes, and they look great for daywear, and glamorous for the evening.

Embellishments—The LBD can feature embellishments, but nothing over the top or too heavy. Beading, lace, chiffon, or sequins are all perfectly acceptable, but only if they, too, are black or in a complementary color, and are used economically rather than cover the whole dress.

Sexiness—One of the most important rules of all is that the LBD has to be sexy but still sophisticated and elegant. The LBD needs to celebrate your curves, showcase your legs, and honor your neckline, shoulders, and arms. However, never try to squeeze into a smaller size than normal, which is so tight that very little is left to the imagination, or raise the hemline to just below the buttocks, as this is not elegant sexiness but instead gives out a very different message.

Investment—It is worth paying a little more for the perfect LBD, as good quality shows. Invest wisely and the dress should last a lifetime (or at least until it no longer fits and you need to reinvest in a new one.)

Versatility—I'm sure you have found yourself staring into the depths of your closet crying, "I have nothing to wear," as you desperately seek something for that special event, only to emerge once again with your old, faithful LBD gripped firmly in your hands. The beauty of the LBD is that it is versatile enough to be worn to almost any occasion, as we'll see in the next section.

How to Wear the LBD

Whether you are seeking a demure daytime look, a stylish ensemble for early evening cocktails followed by dinner, or even a show-stopping dress in which to dance the night away, the LBD is an ideal choice. It's all a question of dressing it up or down and choosing the right accessories for the look you wish to achieve.

For example, say you are dressing for an important work meeting and then need to attend an event in the evening. For the day look, team the LBD with a stylish tailored jacket, a simple string of pearls (as Chanel intended,) opaque pantyhose, and a pair of court shoes to give you the perfect business outfit. You can take the look from day to evening simply by replacing the pearls with a glitzy necklace, jazzing up the jacket with a sparkling brooch, and replacing the opaque pantyhose with a pair covered in motifs.

Afternoon tea has suddenly become in vogue again, so what better outfit to wear while eating finger sandwiches and delicious cupcakes than your simple smart/casual LBD. Dress it up just enough with some flashy costume jewelry that will get you noticed, but don't go over the top or you'll be noticed for all the wrong reasons.

If you are going to a dinner dance, wear a sparkling shrug or a faux fur jacket over your LBD. Choose a necklace and earrings that make a big statement and finish off the look with a pair of killer heels. It is not imperative that you stick to black shoes—in fact, introducing vibrantly colored shoes that pick up a shade in your necklace will dramatize your look.

For a more exclusive evening engagement, you need to look elegant and refined. You can achieve this by accessorizing your LBD with precious jewelry (diamonds are a girl's best friend,) glimmering skyscraper heels, and a matching clutch purse. Always keep a pair of flat pumps in your bag for walking to the car after a night out—your feet may hurt after wearing high heels for several hours.

Remember, one elegant LBD is all you need, as it will serve you well for any occasion, even a sad one. Although black now has a wide appeal, it is still associated with mourning, so worn with a black wool overcoat and perhaps a pill-box hat and veil, the LBD is the perfect outfit to wear to a funeral.

The World's Most Famous LBD

The LBD has become so iconic that now some dresses are just as famous as the stars who wore them. The most acclaimed is perhaps Hubert de Givenchy's design for actress Audrey Hepburn when she played the character of Holly Golightly in the 1961 movie "Breakfast at Tiffany's". This simple, full-length dress had a shift-style top with a cut-out back detail. Hepburn accessorized the dress with a rhinestone tiara, a heavy pearl necklace, elbow-length black satin gloves, and oversized sunglasses. Although I mentioned earlier that the LBD should ideally be calf-length or shorter (see page 15), this is certainly an exception to the rule, as Hepburn looks absolutely stunning standing outside

Tiffany's in this beautiful dress, eating a croissant from a paper bag. The only LBD to have gone down in the fashion history books as one of the world's most famous dresses, the exquisite creation worn by Hepburn sold at auction in 2006 for $615,000 (£410,000.)

Caring for Your LBD

It may be highly unlikely that your dress would ever reach dizzy heights financially, but that is no excuse for not caring properly for your LBD. A precious fashion commodity, it will be your friend for life if you look after it well.

❉ Always check the care instructions on your garment, as an LBD of good quality will almost certainly be labeled dry clean only. If this is the case, never be tempted to put it in the washing machine because it's unlikely that the dress will come out the same shape and size. Of course, dry-cleaning is not cheap, but surely your invaluable LBD is worth every penny.

❉ If you do happen to have a dress that can be washed, make sure you wash and iron it inside out. Some black fabrics can become shiny when ironed and if you do not iron the reverse side of the material, you could find the dress covered in horrible iron marks that can never be removed.

❉ When storing your dress, it's best to keep it in the closet but not inside a plastic bag, as mildew and mold can get in and cause damage to the fabric as well as creating an unpleasant odor. You can, however, purchase zip-up suit bags that are perfect for keeping your favorite dress free from harm, but do check your closet regularly to make sure that damp hasn't started to appear.

Chapter 2

The Dress

Aside from the LBD, every stylish woman will, of course, own a number of other dresses in various styles, colors, and designs. The most prolific staple among all our garments, the dress is an ideal choice for every possible event, especially when your day demands more color than the LBD can offer or if the occasion is slightly more flamboyant. The dress is the perfect garment for showcasing your personality; it can reveal your emotions, mood, hopes, and ambitions, as well as your passions, simply through its style, color, and fabric.

———•———

Centuries of the Dress

As far back as the ancient civilizations, the dress has dominated women's fashion. In Roman times married women wore a long stola, a type of tunic dress, which was also the favored garment style for females throughout the Saxon period. Made of linen it was worn under a heavier woollen or linen garment. The same style was still popular in the Norman era, the only slight difference being that the overdress was shorter. During the reign of Elizabeth I of England, the farthingale was fashionable. This consisted of a fitted bodice and a wide, full-length skirt supported by hoops. The "Sack Back" was in vogue in the 1700s and displayed broad pleats falling down from the shoulders at the back of the dress.

Georgian fashion revisited ancient Greek and Roman styles, becoming known as Neo-classical. Women wore white muslin, floor-length dresses, which splayed out from a tight bust line and were decorated with glass beadwork. The Regency women revived elaborate decoration and the natural waistline, while early Victorian ladies returned once more to plainer clothing with a corset and many petticoats under the skirt before the introduction of the crinoline (either padded or caged) and then later, the bustle (a wire frame), which was worn under the dress to accentuate drapes at the back and on the hips.

It wasn't until the twentieth century that women's fashion became more varied, innovative, and diverse. High society was largely responsible for the ever-changing fashions throughout the decades, but music and film also influenced the way people dressed, as did the fashion designers themselves. Women gradually became more liberated and, as a result, had more control of their lives, their choices, and their finances. Those in the fashion industry responded to this newfound freedom by constantly striving to create innovative new dress shapes, as well as experimenting with fabrics and embellishments.

In the first half of the century, made-to-measure haute couture (high fashion) was the only way to acquire good-quality dresses and women either had to pay or alternatively make their own at home. World War II shortages instilled in them the attitude that they should "make do and mend," as materials were scarce and clothing rationed. However from the 1950s onward, fashion became more readily available as the couture market went into decline and mass production took over.

This shift in the way clothes were manufactured gave designers the opportunity to produce less expensive pieces on a larger scale. It also meant that women could more easily afford to buy several outfits. As a result clothes began to take on a more evocative feel, with designers re-working historic styles by adding contemporary twists, as well as introducing completely fresh ideas. "New woman" responded eagerly to the exciting new fashions because they were practical, feminine, and ground breaking.

The dress was an item of clothing that underwent the biggest change in the twentieth century, as long, wide, heavy skirts were banished, and replaced by simple silhouettes in shorter lengths. Today these designs are still very much in fashion and can be found in every style-seeking woman's wardrobe.

Dress Style Staples

The dress can be your most powerful fashion tool—if you choose it wisely, it can be a style statement that creates a huge impact. Let's look at some of the most interesting, and influential, dress styles.

The Shift

The most popular of all the dress designs, the shift has become one of our staples, as it possesses a timeless silhouette. It was a favorite style of the young, rebellious "flapper girls" in the 1920s, because it was comfortable to wear, flattering, and perfect for dancing the Charleston in. Originally this dress had a straight silhouette, falling loose from the shoulders to just above the knee. There was no visible waistline and the way in which it skimmed the hips went well with the boyish styles of the "Jazz" era. The shift evolved from its original shape to become more fitted on the hips but still loose at the waist. Appealing to most women, this boxy design comes in every possible fabric, and is available in all colors and patterned prints. The shift dress is an enduring classic that works well for both work engagements and social events.

The Smock

Dating back to the eighteenth century, this shapeless dress was common wear for those working in rural industries. Smocks were made from heavy, durable fabrics, such as wool, and were comfortable

In 1957 fashion designers Givenchy and Balenciaga created a shapeless dress that was known as the "Sack Dress" because it did not accentuate the female figure.

and warm to wear when working outdoors in all weathers. Over the decades the style has evolved and it is now being created from lightweight fabrics, such as cotton. These days featuring embroidery or other embellishments, it is more attractive than earlier versions and is ideal as casual wear, especially if you want to hide your bottom, stomach, and hips. It is also a favorite style for pregnant women.

The Tunic

Another style that looks fantastic on all women, the tunic dress is one of the most ancient of designs because, as already mentioned (see page 22), it was a popular style with both men and women in ancient Greece and Rome. Another loose-fitting garment, although slightly more tailored than the smock, it falls above the knees, and comes in varied sleeve styles and lengths. Again versatile for any occasion, the tunic has become a fashion highlight of late and can be worn either as a short dress or over pants teamed with a pair of heels to give a more sophisticated look.

Wear a dress with draped material down the front if you wish to hide your stomach.

The Wrap

This style first made an appearance in the 1970s when fashion designer Diane von Fürstenberg created a knitted jersey wrap dress. It is perfect for more voluptuous women as its V-neck style with a tight bodice and loose skirt accentuates the bust, slims the waist, and flattens the stomach. Available in a variety of fabrics from silk to cotton and jersey to linen, this is a dress that can be smartened up for the office or dressed down for a walk in the park.

The Bodycon or Tube

A 1980s throwback (not the most flattering fashion era) only the slimmest of women shine in a bodycon dress because, unlike the wrap, this design highlights every inch of the body. Worn like a second skin, it is very tight and is generally created from stretchy material, such as lycra or viscose mix, or some other figure-hugging material. Although it is the ultimate party dress, the bodycon design is really geared to young women and no self-respecting forty-something would dream of squeezing into this provocative dress unless she has a figure to die for.

The Shirt Dress

This type of garment is as it sounds: a simple button-down-the-front dress, often made from shirt-like fabrics, such as cotton. It first came into fashion during the 1950s and remained popular throughout the 1960s. Originally known as a "shirtwaister," this style needs a belt to define the waist, with the skirt varying in length and style. Shirt dresses are simple yet very smart, and work well as office wear. However, some fashion designers have jazzed up the design, making this kind of dress suitable for evening wear when teamed with a few extravagant accessories.

The Vintage Style

Retro is back! The 1950s circle-skirted dress and the '60s mini are incredibly in vogue with those who appreciate vintage fashion. In fact, many designers take inspiration from these influential decades and re-work the popular fashions of the day into contemporary styles. Choose between a genuine, original, vintage dress for a one-off ensemble or go for a modern "vintage" style, which can be just as effective in portraying your desired fashion statement. Ensure, though, that when purchasing a vintage dress, you choose a design that is evocative of a particular era—for example, poodle and Scottie dog motifs that reflect the 1950s or psychedelic or Op-art prints for the 1960s. (For more on vintage fashion, see Chapter 9.)

Buying authentic vintage dresses will not only enhance your wardrobe but also ensure that you will never be caught in that embarrassing situation where you turn up to an event only to find that someone else is wearing an identical dress.

The Tea Dress

Ditsy, floral, and feminine the tea dress evokes the 1940s. Although it is available in many styles, it is usually short, with capped or short sleeves and a full skirt. Perfect for those who love an afternoon tea dance or just a lazy row along the river, this dress conjures up visions of simple bygone times and so should be worn for enjoyable, leisurely activities.

The Maxi

Very on-trend recently, the maxi first caught the fashionable public's eye in 1967, but became a firm fashion must-have throughout the 1970s. With an ankle- or floor-length skirt that either drops from under the bust line or the waist, this dress can have many types of sleeves and is a popular choice for wearing on sun-drenched holidays, because it is cool both in terms of being practical in a warm climate and stylish in the fashion stakes.

The Cut

Different cuts of dress can either enhance your body shape or highlight imperfections, so choose a flattering style. If you have a fuller figure, wear tailored pieces that give definition to the waist. Never wear frills and keep your dress silhouette streamlined. Women who have a curvy, hourglass shape should opt for dresses cut on the bias, as these cling to accentuate the figure, while those with a boyish physique should always define the waist and wear a V-shaped neckline to create a bust.

Color Association

Color has always played an important role when it comes to dressing correctly for particular engagements or events. We are all aware that black is appropriate for funerals and that navy, brown, and gray are acceptable colors to wear when attending a corporate interview. But there are also many trendy shades, which every fashionista has to be seen wearing at the beginning of the season, for example when "lime green is the new black!"

Color can also reflect your mood and your personality, or represent your standing in society. For example, purple has always been regarded as majestic and red is seen as loud and dangerous, while sky blue is perceived as calm and honest. Think carefully, when picking your dress, which color will help you to make the statement you are trying to convey. If you want to stand out and be noticed, then red is definitely for you, whereas if you prefer a more demure appearance, choose a dress in what Barbara Hulanicki, owner of 1960s–70s London boutique Biba, referred to as "aunties' colors"—mauves, browns, plums, and rusts.

Don't be afraid to combine vibrant colors—for example, you could match up bright orange with cerise pink, or purple with turquoise. Color blocking has become the latest craze in fashion and does actually look fantastic. Apparently, "blue and green should never been seen, except with something in between," but wearing a vibrant blue dress with an equally vivid green jacket will harmonize your look, as long as you are still cutting a great edge in style.

Prince of Prints

If plain-Jane block colors aren't your thing, why not home in on one of the amazing array of dresses with prominent prints or patterns. Florals, tribal patterns, geometric prints, and stripes are among the more common ones and are all found in a huge range of dress styles.

The one thing you need to remember when buying dresses emblazoned with prints is that not all of them work for everybody, so make sure you try your dress on and are happy with it before purchasing it. Otherwise, it could be condemned to the closet for eternity, never to see the light of day.

Start with a small, all-over print design because this is easier to wear than larger patterns. Then, once you are confident with your choices, you can get a little more adventurous by wearing bigger prints. Also smaller, all-over prints can flatter your figure, while larger prints can highlight parts of your body you don't necessarily want to draw attention to, so be particular when choosing a patterned dress.

Never wear fussy "statement" accessories with a print dress. In fact, if you have picked your dress

Wear prints with pride, but just give an extra thought to which one will best suit your personality and your body shape, as well as complement the dress's style.

well, you shouldn't require jewelry—just a plain pair of shoes and matching purse should suffice. The print is all you need to grab attention.

Petite floral prints look great on maxi dresses, especially if you highlight the most prominent color from the print and match it up with an oversized 1970s-style floppy felt hat. Finish off with a pair of thonged, jeweled sandals or flip flops and you will look cool, calm, and collected in the summer months.

Geometric prints, especially those inspired by the Art Deco era, are

If you like wearing stripes, the rule is that horizontal stripes make you look wider, while vertical stripes give you a slimmer appearance.

best suited to shift dresses. As already mentioned (see page 24,) this was the favored shape during this vibrant era and still is the perfect silhouette for carrying off bold prints. When you wear a shift dress with a pair of Mary Janes, or bar shoes, you will be replicating one of the most stylish periods of the twentieth century. What better outfit is there to party in?

British designer Holly Fulton is inspired by all things Art Deco, a fact that she displays through the stylish prints on her dresses. Expensive but desirable, Fulton's designs are the perfect option for those who wish to stand out in original designs.

Material Matters

Every possible type of material has been made into a dress over the decades, including the truly bizarre, such as metal, paper, plastic, and even cardboard. In general, though, women do prefer to wear more conventional fabrics, some of which are made from natural fibers, the others from synthetic fibers. Textured fabrics can be either natural or synthetic. Here are some examples of popular fabrics for dresses:

* Natural: Silk, linen, cotton, cashmere, and wool

* Synthetic: Polyester, rayon, nylon, viscose, acetate, denim, and acrylic

* Textured: lace, velvet, and quilted

Fabrics made from natural fibers are always best. They are generally more expensive than synthetic materials, but they are of a high quality and they also feel better against the skin than some synthetic fabrics.

You also need to consider how flattering these fabrics will be to your figure. If you are of a bigger build, avoid clinging wool and tight stretchy textiles, although if the dress is draped, pliable jersey materials can hide a multitude of sins. Free-flowing fabrics that skim, such as silk and cotton, are perfect for women with a fuller figure.

If you have a more boyish shape, try textured lace and velvet fabrics, made with natural fibers, to add dimension, but cotton, satin, and silk are also ideal for slimmer figures.

Sparkling Sensation

When it comes to exciting nights out you will want to add a touch of sparkle to your dress. Sequins, glitter, faux gemstones, and rhinestones adorn dresses in every shape, size, and length. Some believe that bling should only be for the younger generations, but I disagree—as long as a dress is tastefully embellished, women of all ages should be allowed to sparkle. The only style rule in my book is that, when wearing these shining ensembles, you ensure that you razzle dazzle the night away!

Famous and Iconic Dresses

Aside from Audrey Hepburn's Givenchy LBD, there are many other memorable dresses that are now considered among the most famous in the world. These include:

✻ The white halter neck dress designed by William Travilla and worn by Marilyn Monroe in the 1955 film "The Seven Year Itch". It was sold in 2011 at auction by actress Debbie Reynolds as part of a collection of film memorabilia for a staggering $4.2m (£2.8m.)

✻ Elizabeth Hurley's Versace safety-pin dress worn at the premier of the film "Four Weddings and a Funeral" in 1994.

✻ The Duchess of Cambridge, Kate Middleton's sheer dress worn in 2002 for a university charity fashion show, which sold for $117,000 (£78,000) in 2010.

✻ Yves Saint Laurent's 1965 Mondrian dress, estimated to be worth $45,000–$60,000 (£30,000-£40,000.)

✳ Andy Warhol 1960s "Souper" paper dress estimated to be worth $1,500–$2,250 (£1,000-£1,500.)

✳ The Elsa Schiaparelli collaboration with surrealist artist Salvadore Dali called the "Lobster" dress, infamously worn by Wallis Simpson, Duchess of Windsor in a series of photographs taken by Cecil Beaton in the 1930s.

Chapter 3

The Pant Suit

Historically, pants (trousers) were regarded as being a masculine form of dress that no lady would ever consider wearing. However, this antiquated attitude was to change dramatically in the first half of the twentieth century when pants became very in vogue among more discerning women. While pants are a relatively modern fashion phenomenon, today times have moved on even further and it is widely accepted that the majority of women own at least one smart, tailored pant suit for daywear and/or a more flamboyant example for evening dress. In fact, the pant suit has become one of the most indispensable outfits a woman can own. It works both as a suit and as separates that can be combined with other pieces. The only rigid requirement is that the suit is in a classic cut that will never date.

———◆———

The Origins of the Pant Suit

During the early to mid-ninteenth century some women wore pants while they worked, because these garments were much more practical than the restrictive long skirts that were fashionable at the time. This scandalized a Victorian society that believed ladies should never be seen in such masculine attire. In fact, this attitude persisted until the early part of the twentieth century when unisex pants became more acceptable if worn for sporting activities. By the 1930s, women's pants had become slightly more popular. However, society wasn't totally ready to understand this shift in gender dressing until the 1970s and even then many employers banned women from wearing any form of pants in the workplace.

Acceptance began just after the Great Depression hit in 1929. The dark economic cloud encouraged people to turn to the silver screen and Hollywood as a form of escapism. Famous actors and actresses of the time were idolized not only for their glamorous lifestyles, but also as leading lights in fashion. German-born actress Marlene Dietrich was one of the most forward when it came to experimenting with clothes, especially as her androgynous persona meant she was often seen sporting masculine attire. It was in the 1930 film "Morocco" that Dietrich was first seen wearing her trademark pant suit, which had bell bottoms, and captured the public's attention. Dietrich was to become the most formidable fashion icon of her time when it came to controversial dress. However, Katharine Hepburn, who was equally famous as an actress, also became renowned for wearing pants, which helped popularize the look even more.

With the outbreak of World War II in 1939 the role of filling in at the workplace while the men were away fighting fell to Britain's women. Much of the work was in munitions factories or on the farms as part of the "land army," so practical clothing was essential.

Women would wear pants because they allowed more freedom of movement, and eventually this resulted in pants for women becoming more widespread and thus acceptable in society.

Fashion designer Yves Saint Laurent famously introduced the "Smoking Tuxedo," the ultimate pant suit for women, in the mid-1960s, proving that women could look just as elegant and sophisticated in a tailored suit as in a dress. Up until this point, the tailored suit had been reserved for men. However, it is believed that British designers Marion Foale and Sally Tuffin were slightly ahead of Laurent when they dressed model Jill Kennington in a corduroy jacket with matching pants. This concept felt a little alien at first and, in fact, made the designers roll around with laughter, because they had never before seen casual female pants teamed with a matching jacket. But the concept worked, the model looked amazing and the pant suit was born.

In 1967 the Duke of Norfolk banned women from wearing pant suits within the Royal Enclosure at Ascot.

For evening, the palazzo pant suit became popular, since it was both comfortable and stylish to wear. The height of fashion from the 1960s into the 1970s, these suits had pants that were set in at the waistline and flowed down into wide legs, giving the illusion of a skirt. Popular in silk fabric, and often embellished or made in vibrant colors, the palazzo pant suit became a show-stopping alternative to the evening gown.

From then on, the women's pant suit became acceptable attire for both daytime and evening. In fact, today there is a vast difference between a man's suit and a woman's pant suit, thus erasing any lingering speculation that women are now wearing something that was once considered male-only clothing. Tailored pant suits are prolific in the office environment, while less structured, glamorous suits work well as evening wear. Available in an assortment of colors, material, and styles, the women's pant suit has become another fashion staple, and in common with the LBD, it can deliver the desired stylish effect on every occasion.

Au Fait with Fashion

As always fashion dictates, but when it comes to the pant suit, again you must ignore fly-by-night fashion fads and invest in something a little more classic. So please avoid wearing your favorite, original 1970s flares down the street, as you could well cause a stir for all the wrong reasons! And don't despair if you can't get into a pair of this season's tight skinny pants—the staple items in your closet will never ever date and so can be worn no matter what the current fashion may be. The same rule applies to the jacket—avoid wide, pointed lapels, which again were popular in the '70s; double-breasted jackets, which were more of a 1980s fashion fad; and short jackets, which come in and fall out of favor regularly.

The best course of action is to purchase a suit that has straight-cut legs, because these tend to be classic styling. The jacket should be single breasted, falling to just below the buttocks. However, blazer-style jackets have become very popular of late and again these never really seem dated.

If your pocket allows it, it's wise to invest in a made-to-measure tailored suit. Designed specifically to your own criteria, it will fit like a glove and, of course, be a one-off, personalized for you.

If you are wanting to update your suit for something trend-setting with an edge of sassiness, buy a high-end designer label, such as Vivienne Westwood, but remember you still need to choose a classic cut.

Conventional Color

Pant suits, in my opinion, need to be conservative in color, especially when it comes to everyday wear. Vibrant orange, red, or green is over-kill and very rarely looks stylish, so stick to the usual gray, black, chocolate brown, navy, camel, and perhaps sage green shades in the winter months. These colors will give you an air of class and sophistication, and add sharpness to your style. For spring and summer, pastel hues, such as baby pink, blue, white, lilac, and lemon, are fresh, clean colors that have a pleasant, sunny feel.

No to Prints

Never wear pant suits made from all-over prints, otherwise you will be making a huge fashion *faux pas*. Even if you feel drawn to bright colors, resist and steer clear of animal prints, florals, bold stripes, and checks. Generally regarded as bad taste, they will not help you achieve your goal of becoming a style sensation, but instead highlight you as a woman who has questionable dress sense.

Versatile and Stylish

As accepted office wear the pant suit has a reputation for being quite dull and conservative, but this doesn't have to be the case. Yes, it's the easiest thing to slip into for work, as it is comfortable, smart, and effective when you want to blend into the office background, but sometimes a statement needs to be made. It is important to own that staple classic in your wardrobe, but why not make an exception to the style rule and buy an additional pant suit that is a little more fashionable, quirky, adventurous, and interesting. It's not going to be a suit that you wear for decades to follow, but it will give you that unusual alternative on days when conventional just doesn't fit your mood.

In the Workplace

Suits should be tailored, fitted for a slim figure, or loose for a larger woman. Dual colors and pin-stripes offer alternatives to the usual plain suit, as do Harris and herringbone tweeds. A shirt in one color worn underneath a pant suit gives a corporate look, while a patterned alternative adds a less serious dimension and lifts a single-colored suit. Camisole vests or blouses soften the overall effect, and for that extra, uber-stylish, gender-bending focus, wear a pair of masculine suspenders (braces.)

Casual Daywear

The majority of women steer clear of wearing tailored pant suits on informal occasions, preferring to project a different image when away from work. However, on hot, sticky, summer days a lightweight linen ensemble, or a pair of wide-legged palazzo pants worn with a loose-fitting, shirt-style jacket, still looks elegant and chic.

The Joys of Separates

Just because you purchased a suit doesn't mean you have to wear the pants and the jacket together all the time. Blazers or "boyfriend" jackets look amazing with jeans or even over a summer teadress. Pants can be worn with a variety of tops or dresses, teamed with stiletto heels, boots, or flat shoes or sandals, depending on the occasion.

Nights Out

In recent decades the pant suit has become popular as evening wear. To carry off this look, again classic design is imperative, but if you want to appear a little more adventurous, there are some excellent alternatives that still deliver that element of style.

Women can carry off a female version of the male tuxedo with grace. Wear it with an elegant female button-up dress shirt (bow tie optional, but remember you still want to look feminine, so I suggest you ditch this accessory) and a pair of killer heels. No longer resembling a masculine form of dress, it's a smart, elegant, and chic way to carry off the traditional tux.

If you prefer to wear something a little more extravagant, which is still the epitome of class, why not consider luxurious fabrics. Velvet, satin, silk, or corduroy can be fun, playful alternatives to conventional suit fabrics. Remember that some of these materials can date, so choose carefully and steer clear of lamé, as this hideous '80s fabric is unlikely ever to come back into fashion!

A black pant suit with a touch of shimmer is the perfect take on the classic suit for a night out, especially if the fabric incorporates silver or gold flecks. Add an oversized sparkling brooch for extra va-va-voom.

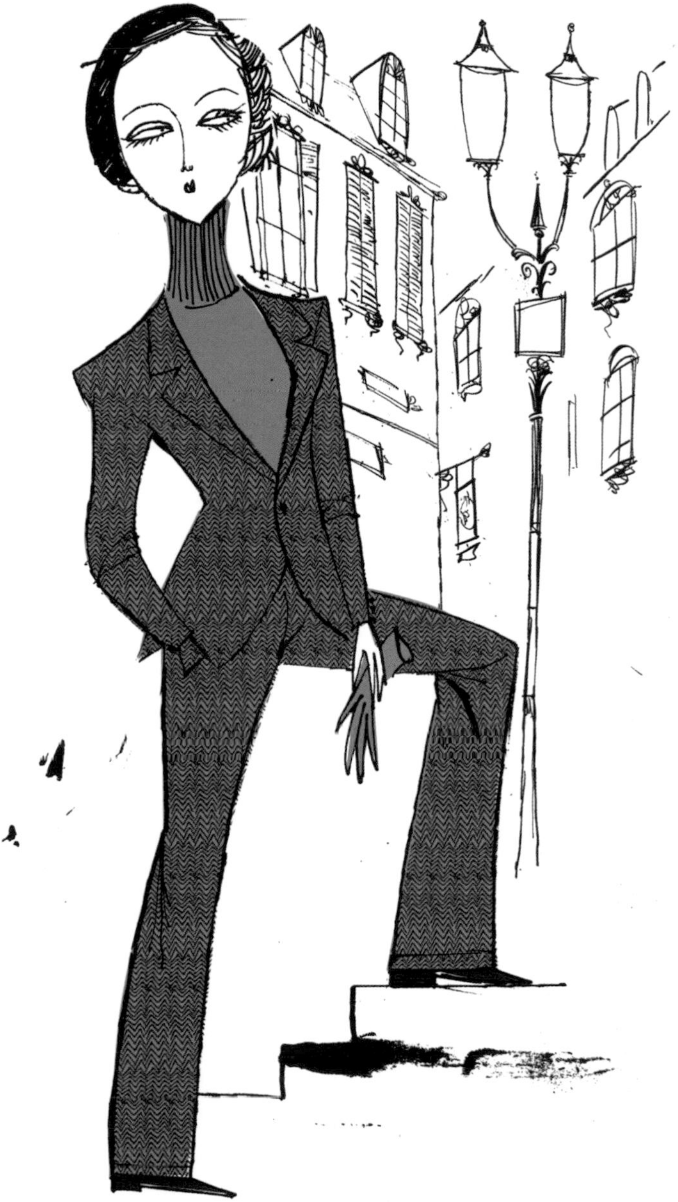

Chapter 4

Shirts, Blouses, and Tops

A large proportion of your wardrobe should consist of separates. Every stylish woman requires a variety of tops in the form of shirts, blouses, T-shirts, and knitwear to wear with her skirts, shorts, and pants. Necessary for projecting a smart–casual image, their appeal is in their versatility—mixing and matching different items of clothing can widen your wardrobe and, if correctly used, create numerous customized looks.

Shirts

A multifaceted piece of clothing, the shirt is a timeless garment that will serve you well for years to come. A white button-down shirt, either fitted at the waist or straight cut, is a must for any wardrobe because it's so versatile. Worn under a blazer with skinny jeans, tucked into a pair of black pants, left loose with a waistcoat, or belted in to accentuate your waist, it's a casual must-have. In a business context the shirt can be worn under a work suit or tucked into a pencil skirt and teamed with a pair of court shoes. Quality is also important as this wardrobe essential will be used often, so the better the fabric the longer it will last. If possible opt for cotton, which is durable, soft, and lightweight, as well as being comfortable to wear.

Originating from the French chemise, shirts were historically made from rough cloth and linen and were worn as undergarments by both sexes.

Blouses

Funky and feminine alternatives to the shirt, blouses are wardrobe essentials that can work well for almost every occasion.

Today, blouses are a far cry from the old-fashioned, dainty, high-necked styles that were so popular in Victorian and Edwardian times. They come in softer fabrics, are loose fitting, and available in a wide array of patterns and designs. Some are sleeveless, others draped, and many display embellishments, while still others have more traditional styling, featuring bows, lace, and ruffles.

The Pussy Bow

This is the most traditional of all the styles. Tying at the neckline, this blouse looks chic under a suit jacket, slightly more edgy when worn with jeans, and oozes sophisticated sexiness if teamed with a pencil skirt. It is usually made from silky materials and is suitable for all seasons. Wear vibrant jewel colors during the drab winter months or on-trend animal prints to brighten up your day.

The Bib

If the pussy bow is a little too girlie for your taste, the perfect alternative could be the bib blouse. Similar to a shirt in design, it has a bib panel at the front in either the same color as the main body or a contrasting shade. Necklines vary from a peter-pan collar to no collar at all. This blouse is suitable for the office environment or alternatively can be worn casually with jeans, pants, or a skirt.

The Smock

This casual blouse has no buttons down the front and no defining waistline. It is very reminiscent of the '70s, especially when featuring embroidery embellishments, and you can carry the retro style through by wearing it with wide-legged palazzo pants. To vary the silhouette, add a belt under the bust line or at the waist.

The Gypsy

Also known as the peasant blouse, this is one of the most popular styles and suits every body type. Classed as bohemian fashion, this blouse is floaty and feminine because it is generally loose at the top and narrows down to become more fitted at the waist. Versatile, it can be worn with pants, maxi or mini dresses, and various types of skirts.

The Cape

The perfect evening blouse, the cape comes in various styles. It can have sleeves, one shoulder, or be sleeveless; it can be cropped and elasticated at the waist or longer in length. Sometimes the cape is detachable. Another possibility is to have bat-wing or, as the name suggests, cape sleeves. Cape blouses most often have a scooped neckline and this design commonly comes in chiffon, silk, or metallic material to enhance its evening appeal.

T-shirts

The T-shirt is one of the more prolific items of clothing in our wardrobes. This simple, basic top comes in either tank style or with short or long sleeves. T-shirts are found in every color and print imaginable, with some displaying slogans or graphic designs. The majority of women own a wide range in different hues because this top complements just about every type of garment. It looks fabulous when layered but also is extremely stylish when worn with a simple pair of jeans.

Owning T-shirts with an assortment of neck lines is a good idea, especially if you like the layered look and want to put, for example, a long-sleeved crew neck under a short-sleeved scooped neck (see page 55.) A particular outfit may demand a T-shirt of a certain cut and shape—for example, a tight-fitting, V-neck tank worn with a long maxi skirt is more striking than a short-sleeved round-necked version.

Another reason this top is so popular and ubiquitous is that it suits everyone and every body shape, irrespective of age. It is also the most comfortable of all garments, generally created from 100 percent cotton or a cotton/polyester mix, as well as being the most versatile. All in all, the T-shirt is a quick style-fix top that works at all times.

During the day

For daywear, team your T-shirt with jeans, a blazer, and either a pair of heels or flat pumps, for an uncomplicated style statement. Alternatively, a long-sleeved T-shirt under a short-sleeved jersey dress worn with opaque pantyhose and chunky boots looks incredibly stylish in the fall.

In the Evening

To look good in the evening, try putting a long, glitzy tank top with a short skirt, motif pantyhose, and a pair of knee-length boots for a perfect party outfit. Or for a dinner engagement, wear your T-shirt with a pair of straight-leg pants, a boyfriend jacket, a pair of heels, and some sparkly jewelry.

Knitwear

Knitwear is essential for those cold winter months. Bulky, oversized sweaters, short, cropped knits, and even the motif Christmas pullover remain all the rage with faithful followers of fashion. These styles make fine additions to your wardrobe, but for your knitwear basics, it's advisable to stick to classic styles that will serve you well year after year.

The Cardigan

Adding the finishing touch to a subtle daytime outfit, the cardigan is one of those essentials that we cannot live without. This knitwear staple is named after James Thomas Brudenell, the 7th Earl of Cardigan, who was also famous for leading the charge of the Light Brigade in 1854 during the Crimean War. A privileged British military commander, he wanted a garment to keep him warm under his uniform, so he took to wearing a knitted vest with buttons. As with any successful invention it caught on quickly and it wasn't long before all the other officers were following Cardigan's lead and wearing similar garments.

The original design was very different from the modern versions we wear today, which began to evolve into the style we know from the Victorian era onward. Over the decades the cardigan has retained its original, practical use—keeping us warm—but has also become a fashion item that can make a trendy style statement.

Aside from the traditional styles with buttons down the front, cardigans can be open or have zipper fasteners. They are available in various woollen materials with cashmere and lambswool being the most desirable and expensive.

Different styles suit different body shapes, so if you have an hourglass figure, opt for a fitted cardigan to enhance your curves, and avoid big, bulky versions. If you are more of a pear shape, balancing your top half with your hips is essential, so choose a style that has broader shoulders. If you are slim, you can create the illusion of curves by wearing a belted cardigan to accentuate your waist.

The Sweater

The rules that apply to cardigans also apply to sweaters. Big and bulky woollen sweaters will certainly keep you warm and, when worn with a scarf, make a stylish alternative to the winter coat. Sweaters made from silk and cotton are perfect for layering over other tops, particularly in the spring and the fall.

Consider carefully which neckline to choose—as sweaters are worn so near to your face it is important to be comfortable. A roll-neck sweater comes up high, just under the chin, while a cowl neck drapes down in folds below the neck. There are many other variants, from the V-neck to the turtle neck, but the standard sweater is the crew neck, which comes up to the base of the neck.

Aran sweaters, with their textured cable patterns, are a good choice when embarking on a country walk in winter or fall. The wool can hold a lot of water before feeling wet should it suddenly start to rain. Originating from a group of islands off the west coast of Ireland, the sweaters used to feature combinations of stitching that were uniquely related to the lives and families of the individuals who created them. They are also known as "fishermen's jumpers." Today many of the Aran-style sweaters on sale are machine made, but these are just as practical for displaying a sense of country chic.

In the past, fishermen who lost their lives at sea were identified through the unique patterns on the Aran sweaters they were wearing.

The Bolero or Shrug

The bolero or shrug acts very much like a contemporary version of the historical shawl. With either short or long sleeves, this cropped garment covers the shoulders and reaches just below the bust line, usually hanging open without a fastening. A chic alternative to the common cardigan, it's perfect for spring and summer as an extra layer or worn for an evening engagement over a dress. Boleros and shrugs come in a host of materials, including silk, lace, and cotton mixtures, but the knitted version is the classic style. Every woman should own a bolero or a shrug in a neutral color, because it's such a versatile garment that can be worn on many important occasions.

Layering Your Tops

Don't be afraid to wear more than one top at a time to give a layered appearance. Suitable for every season of the year, this look gives a more interesting vibe to your style and extends your wardrobe choices. Experiment by combining shades of color and prints, different lengths, styles, and sleeve types. Begin with simple layered outfits, otherwise the result could look cluttered and bulky. For example, in winter you could wear a jewel-colored, plain, cropped knitted tank top or a round-necked sweater with short sleeves over a white or dark shirt. For for spring try putting a tight-fitting, long-sleeved T-shirt under a floaty, short-sleeved gypsy-style top or even a day dress for a stylish effect.

Once you are feeling more confident with your layering, try mixing plain colors with flirty florals or dramatic prints. A chintzy or geometric patterned vest top worn over another plain and slightly longer top reveals layering at the hemline. Add a bolero, a shrug, or a cardigan in a subtle, complementary shade and wear them with plain pants or a short skirt for a fresh spring or summer ensemble that has great impact.

When layering, don't be afraid to mix and match necklines—for example, try a V-neck over a scooped neck or a roll neck under a square neck.

Wear a long T-shirt or a tank top beneath a short cape blouse that has an elasticated, gathered hemline at the waist for a glamorous evening look when going out for drinks and dinner with the girls.

Chapter 5

The Skirt

Aside from the dress, the other garment that can make the biggest fashion statement is the skirt. An all-important separate, this versatile article of clothing can instantly transform your image from one of authoritative sophistication to bohemian free-spiritedness, or from stylish elegance to alluring sexiness. The skirt is a garment that has changed dramatically over time and has created much controversy in society, playing a significant role in the liberation of women and becoming one of the most influential items of fashion in the twentieth century.

History in Brief

With a few exceptions, skirts have historically been long, covering most if not all of a woman's legs, and hence up until the early twentieth century they flowed down to the floor. It was only when the Jazz Age of the 1920s arrived that the hemline steadily became shorter, beginning with a rise to calf length and gradually creeping up above the knee. This was seen as provocative and shocked the older generations who believed that women's legs should remain covered for modesty's sake. However, the pioneers who dared to adopt this revolutionary new length soon realized that it not only gave them greater ease of movement, but it was also incredibly sexy, and could look elegant and stylish, too. It is hardly surprising then that the short skirt of the 1920s was responsible for the demise of the restrictive longer length, becoming the first of many modern styles that were to appear in the decades to follow.

The '50s Circle

Fashion designer Christian Dior was the innovator behind two of our most famous skirt styles (see The Pencil, below.) His first collection "Corolla," which was shown in 1947, consisted of dresses with tight bodices and vast skirts with petticoats, a style that was to become a hallmark of 1950s fashion.

This style is still popular today, although nowadays women wear a slimmer version without all the petticoats underneath, often in the form of cocktail dresses. Some refer to it as the "ballet" style and it remains one of the most elegant of all skirt styles.

The Pencil

Seven years after introducing the "New Look," Dior finally moved away from this feminine and elegant style by introducing the "Flat Look," which was reminiscent of the boyish silhouette of the 1920s. In this style the waistline was once more dropped to the hips and busts were again flattened, the idea being to promote a straight silhouette. This gave birth to a classic straight skirt—what is now recognizable as the 1950s pencil skirt.

One of the most sophisticated skirt styles, the straight, tight, figure-hugging pencil skirt instantly conveys chic, class, and elegance. Its clean, narrow-fitting silhouette hugs the hips, bottom, and thighs before finishing with a hemline that falls just on or below the knee. Very flattering to those with a slender bodyline, this skirt can also be worn by women with a larger frame. However, this is where the choice of material is crucial—larger women should opt for more rigid fabrics, which will not cling to every curve.

Very popular today with those who work in an office environment, or who like to look chic, this is a skirt that has never really gone out of fashion.

The Mini

A favorite since its creation in the 1960s, the word "mini" refers to the short length of the skirt, which is always above the knee. British designer Mary Quant is usually credited with the introduction of the mini skirt. However, some believe that John Bates, who designed under the name Jean Varon, was actually the first to create this short version of the skirt. Regardless of who first introduced this style, the mini skirt has remained one of the boldest fashion statements of its time. The mini skirt started out at just above knee length but, as time went on, it became shorter and shorter until it finally came to mean a skirt that rested just below the buttocks on the thigh. The most prolific style of the 1960s, it is still one of the most popular skirts of all with young women.

Of course, only courageous girls with fantastic legs can carry off very short minis, and in general this type of skirt should be reserved for the young generation. However, that's not to say that a more mature woman can't ever wear a mini skirt—it just means that you have to be honest with yourself and know your body. If you have any doubts that you can wear a shorter length with style—don't!

Often worn as part of an evening outfit, the mini skirt is a great choice for going clubbing or to a party. The skirt also looks good during the day with pantyhose, which is exactly how it was worn during the swinging '60s.

The Midi

Women who were uncomfortable wearing the mini in the 1960s opted for a longer length that extended below the knee, known as the midi. Still seen as provocative, it showed just enough of the leg to be enticing. Again one of the lengths popular in today's fashion circles, the midi looks especially elegant if worn in the form of a straight-cut wrap skirt in jersey or with a slightly fuller skirt for those with a more pear-shaped figure.

The Maxi

Hemlines went full circle back toward the end of the 1960s, and floor-length maxi skirts were the norm in the 1970s. Less restrictive than previous long skirts, the material was lighter and more free-flowing.

Once again the maxi has returned and is ideal for wearing in summer. The style is suitable for any body shape, although it doesn't suit shorter women and is more effective on those who are taller.

The A-Line

This skirt is fitted at the hips, gradually widening out as it falls in the shape of an "A" The silhouette was dubbed the "New Look" by the Editor-in-Chief of *Harpers & Queen* magazine when Dior first unveiled it. A skirt is usually termed A-line if it makes the hips appear wider than the bust. Maintaining its popularity throughout the 1960s and 1970s, this skirt completely disappeared from the fashion scene in the 1980s when straighter styles

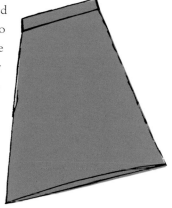

were in vogue. The recent renewed interest in vintage fashion and retro looks has encouraged the return of the A-line skirt, although contemporary versions tend to be less wide in shape than those from previous decades.

The slight A-line is often a popular choice for mature women, who like to dress comfortably. This skirt is also perfect for hiding a bulging stomach or large hips.

The Tulip

A relatively new style, the tulip is narrow at the waist and blooms out on the hips, tapering in again at the hemline. This is an unusual shape and only those with a boyish figure can really carry it off with style, as it over-accentuates the hip and bottom areas.

The Bodycon or Tube

Very much as it sounds, the bodycon or tube is a tight-fitting skirt in a stretchy fabric, similar to the bodycon or tube dress. This is the ideal skirt to wear over opaque pantyhose in the winter teamed with a shorter top, but it should only ever be worn by those who have a slight frame.

Peplums

A peplum is an alternative way to add dimension to an otherwise straight, simple line. Normally reserved for adding to dresses, the peplum is a flourish of fabric sewn at the hip, and it has suddenly come back into fashion on skirts and jackets. Some peplums are flared, thus accentuating the hip area; others are tight-fitting, emphasizing the waist. It really depends on the cut of the dress, skirt, or jacket whether or not a peplum will add style, but you should consider it if you are looking for unusual ways to create interest in an otherwise straight skirt line.

Skirt Styling

In summary, every skirt style and length can look good if teamed with the ideal top and worn in a way that complements your body shape, but here are a few styling suggestions. The structured pencil skirt demands a blouse, a shirt, or a sweater to give it a sophisticated edge, while the mini is more flirtatious and fun and so should be worn with equally fun fashion tops. The maxi shines in the summer when worn as a gypsy skirt with a V-neck tank top, while the fuller A-line skirt is a flattering alternative, especially if worn with a bustier top.

If you are wearing a patterned skirt, wear it with a plain top for a high-impact, stylish look.

Available in almost every material, and a variety of prints, patterns, and colors, skirts come in a huge range of guises—some are plain, others are pleated, and still others display sexy splits up the sides or the back. The only real style rule for skirts is that you choose your coordinating tops and accessories with care. Every wardrobe should contain the basic essentials—a pencil skirt, a mini, and a maxi—in order to ensure you have a design to fit every occasion. However, if you feel uncomfortable in any of these styles, the slight A-line is a great alternative.

Chapter 6

Shoes

Shoes are among our most prized accessories,
adding that all-important finishing touch to every
outfit. Available in a breathtaking variety of styles,
designs, and heights, they have evolved over the
centuries to become one of our most dramatic
fashion statements. They are often the focal point of
a total look, so it is imperative that you choose your
heels (or flats) with care—they must always work in
harmony with your clothes even if your shoes need
to make a louder, stand-alone impression. From
modest to outrageous, brightly colored to somber,
and from six-inch (15cm) stilettos to completely flat
sandals and boots, there is a shoe to fit every foot
and a design to suit every taste.

———◆———

The Origins of the Shoe

Originally created from bark, grass, and vine leaves, shoes protected
our ancestors' feet from the elements as well the dangers of walking
around barefoot. In ancient civilizations they also came to represent
social standing in the community, with only the most affluent women
being able to afford good-quality footwear. Shoes have inspired a

wealth of designs down through the centuries. Nowadays, aside from becoming much more affordable, they are not only regarded as a practical necessity, but in some cases have also become creative works of art for adorning the feet.

In seventeenth-century Britain members of the upper classes wore six-inch (15cm) heels and needed a servant either side to hold them upright.

In fact, shoe design has become such big business that many designers constantly push the boundaries by coming up with the most outrageous designs. Some are practical and can be worn, while others would look more at home displayed in a gallery. One such example is the "Armadillo 10" stiletto designed by the late, great Alexander McQueen for his Spring 2010 collection and worn by Lady Gaga in her "Bad Romance" pop video. Resembling lobster claws, these shoes look impossible to walk in and certainly wouldn't be found in any sensible woman's wardrobe unless, of course, she bought them as an investment and not actually to wear.

With thousands of footwear styles to choose from, there is no reason why you can't have a few pairs that are more elaborate than conventional shoes. These days it is easy to find footwear that is not only stylish and looks fabulous but is also comfortable and has heels you can actually walk in.

Currently, the world's most expensive shoes retail at $210,000 (£140,000.) Created by British jewelry designer Christopher Michael Shellis for the House of Borgezie, they are made from solid gold encrusted with over 2,200 brilliant-cut diamonds, totaling 30 carats.

Shoe and Heel Styles

Court Shoes

The court shoe is the most conservative and classic of all shoe designs. First appearing in the 1860s, it was flat and much like the ballet pump we wear today. Proliferating from the mid-twentieth century onward, this plain style has evolved and is now available with various heel sizes. Often worn by those who work in the business sector, it is ideal for taking you through the day and on into the evening since it complements almost any outfit. This is the staple shoe style that every woman should own.

Peep-toes

These consist of court shoes or sandals with an opening at the toes. Very much for evening occasions, they are classed as "dress shoes." Available in a variety of materials from leather to suede and even in fabric, peep-toes are glamorous classics, combining a staple style with a touch of razzmatazz. Do make sure that before you wear this particular style of shoe, you have a professional pedicure or at the very least paint your toenails—there is nothing worse than displaying ugly, uncared-for toes through the peep-toes.

Stilettos

The slender stiletto heel first made an appearance in the 1930s, although it has often been attributed to shoe designer Roger Vivier, who revived "the little dagger" as it came to be known, during the 1950s. Today this heel style is one of our most popular. It draws attention to the leg and calf, and thus stiletto heels are regarded as the sexiest of shoes. Wearing a stiletto heel is an art, because its height (averaging from four to five inches (10–13cm) can make walking difficult. Some women describe their skyscraper heels as "restaurant shoes," because it is only possible to walk from the car to their table and back again after they have finished their meal. However, others are able to balance on their stilettos all night without flinching. Certainly one of the most elegant styles of footwear, you can't help but feel feminine when wearing a pair and this is why these killer heels are so popular.

Platforms

Music has always influenced the way we dress and with the '70s glam-rock music came the rather impractical and exuberant platform shoe. Of late this style has become fashionable again, although current designs have not quite reached the dizzy heights of the original 1970s shoes. Usually having a five-inch (13cm), chunky heel along with platform soles measuring between one and two inches (2.5–5cm,) these shoes are based on the designs of court shoes, peep-toes, or strappy sandals. Today's version of the platform can also have a stiletto heel with just the sole being more solid. Again very much evening footwear, these shoes look stunning with a mini dress or pants, although for an authentic '70s look they should be worn with a long, flowing, formal evening gown.

Wedges

Ideal for summer, the solid wedge heel is attached to the sole of the shoe. Wedges were invented by the renowned shoe designer Salvatore

Ferragamo in 1936 after he experimented with materials such as wood and cork because of a shortage of leather. This continued throughout World War II, and during the 1940s many women wore this exciting new shoe style, but it was in the 1970s that the wedge became most fashionable. It made a brief re-appearance in the 1990s and then finally came back in vogue at the beginning of the twenty-first century. Today, wedges are one of our staple shoe designs and are worn by women on a regular basis. They are available in various fabrics, colors, and patterns, with the wedge itself commonly created from cork or raffia. They are comfortable shoes to wear, easier to balance on than some other heels, and they offer more support than the stiletto.

Flats

These are definitely not the style to wear on a glamorous night out (and to be honest, flat shoes are rarely flattering for most occasions,) but we all need to own a few pairs for practicality's sake and so that our feet get rested from heels occasionally. Flat shoes go well with summer clothes, so this is the season when they tend to look most stylish. A maxi dress, a mini, and shorts can all make a great statement when teamed with flat pumps or flip flops. Some women wear flats with skinny jeans and the shoes can look good, although not as elegant as heeled shoes, even if they are jazzed up with leopard prints, sparkles, or have big bows on the front.

Boots

The boot first became popular in—and continued to be the most prolific form of footwear throughout—the nineteenth century. Worn by both men and women, the Blucher boot is perhaps the most well-known style from that time, with its open front tab and lacing. Elasticated boots, button boots, cloth boots and the famous Balmoral boots were also favorites with women during this time.

Today, we have an overwhelming selection, as every possible design has been turned into a woman's boot. Choose from thigh-length, knee-high, calf or ankle boots in a huge array of colors, patterns, and heel types. Some lace up the front, others zip up, many have to be pulled on, and some have buckles as fastenings. The choice is very much a personal one, but a pair of black, knee-high boots is a good bet, since this is a style that works well with most outfits.

Quality Not Quantity

Many women own a collection of shoes of which Imelda Marcos would have been proud, as many of us are guilty of popping out to buy one thing only to return clutching a new pair that we spotted in the sale. Men don't understand this fascination with footwear. They tend to treat shoes as functional rather than fashion items, dividing them roughly into their everyday pairs and their "best" pair(s) for social events. As we all know, many females have a compulsive shoe fetish that has to be satisfied!

But whether you are obsessed with acquiring as many pairs of shoes as your wardrobe (or partner) will allow, or only buy shoes when you purchase a new outfit, always buy the best shoes you can afford. The more expensive they are, the better quality (and less likely to hurt your feet) they will be. Remember that well-made shoes last a lifetime. If you can, invest in top-designer styles, such as Manolo Blahnik's elegant stilettos, Vivienne Westwood's pirate boots, or Christian Louboutin's court-shoe platforms, as these high-end, classic designs will be sure to enhance your style status.

Materials

The majority of good-quality shoes are made from leather and really these are the only ones that should adorn your feet. An abundance of plastic shoes is also available, but these shoes are renowned for being uncomfortable to wear, causing blisters, and falling apart. Normally, I would recommend that you stay away from any plastic shoes. However, one particular shoe manufacturer, Melissa, has created eco-friendly plastic PVC footwear that has gone down a storm in the fashion marketplace. Produced by Brazilian company Grendene, these shoes are molded and so they are flexible, comfortable, and design-led—they even smell of bubblegum!

Dramatic Heels

Heels that make a dramatic statement are all the rage at the moment, with many being worked into crazy designs, encrusted with faux stones, or even appearing in unusual shapes. These are perfect if you intend to get noticed when walking on the red carpet or stepping out at an extravagant event. However, style is also very much about subtle statements, so what better way to project this than through a pair of plain shoes that have creative and artistic heels.

Colorful Feet

Of late, brightly colored shoes have become fashionable, especially when worn with black opaque or motif pantyhose. Vibrant reds, pinks, blues, and purples dazzle, and even yellow skyscraper heels can add a wicked sense of fun to a fairly plain outfit.

Of course, the classic black, brown, navy, and neutral colors are still very much in demand for a more demure, businesslike look that is perfect for the office or an important meeting. For women's work shoes the best designs are court shoes and Mary Janes, as these project an image of being organized, tidy, and efficient yet quietly stylish.

Sparkles, glitter, studs, and sequins in silver, bronze, and gold are ideal for a night out and are guaranteed to get you noticed. These statement shoes need to have five-inch (13cm) killer heels and can vary in design from courts to peep-toes to strappy sandals. The only shoes to be seen in when dancing the night away, they are described as "killer heels" for a reason, so make sure you have a pair of comfortable flat pumps in your bag; otherwise any walking afterward could be extremely painful.

Lazy summer days and vacations are ideal for showcasing shoes in more subtle pastel hues, with wedges, ballerina pumps, and flip flops being the footwear of choice.

Patterns and Prints

Animal prints are back with a vengeance and this time they are not cheap or tasteless, but when worn correctly can look very stylish. The rule is not to overdo it but to enhance your outfit by displaying a touch of print rather than covering yourself with it from head to toe. A pair of leopard-print killer heels and a matching clutch purse worn with an LBD looks stunning, either for a night out with the girls or even for a business meeting.

Brighten up an outfit that presents a single block of color by complementing it with a pair of shoes that has a pattern or a print in an identical hue.

Shoes ... Shoes ... and More Shoes

Wearing fanciful footwear is one of the most fun things you can do with fashion, so enjoy hunting out those quirky designs and wear them proudly. Always be mindful of the occasion as plain classics are still expected when you are wearing a business suit or smart working attire, but when you are at leisure and feeling playful, display your more extravagant, embellished, and colored heels with pride. Guaranteed to get you noticed, these attention-seeking shoes are the ultimate statement when showcasing your own unique style.

"The shoe is very much an x-ray of social comportment."
Christian Louboutin, shoe designer

Famous Shoes

* The ruby-red slippers worn by Judy Garland in the 1939 movie, "The Wizard of Oz" sold at Christies East in New York City on May 24, 2000 for $666,000 (£444,000.)

* Marilyn Monroe's white Salvatore Ferragamo strappy sandals worn with her halter-neck dress in the film "The Seven Year Itch," form an iconic image of the actress.

* Vivienne Westwood's "Super Elevated Gilles" worn by supermodel Naomi Campbell on the catwalk in 1993 will never be forgotten because the supermodel toppled over in them.

Caring for Your Shoes

* On buying an expensive pair of shoes, always visit the shoe menders and ask for sole protectors and rubber tips to be applied before you wear them. This ensures that the delicate leather never wears out on the soles and the heels have added insurance.

* Women's shoes don't need polishing frequently unless they are made of black, navy, or brown leather. If they are made of a more delicate material, such as canvas or suede, invest in a spray shoe protector, so that rain or any drink spillage doesn't damage the shoe.

* Have your shoes mended regularly.

* Don't wear good-quality leather or suede in the rain or snow, because watermarks will ruin them. Instead, invest in a pair of rubber boots to wear in bad weather.

✻ If your shoes are supplied with a protective bag on purchase, store them in the bag away from sunlight, damp, and dust.

✻ Never throw your shoes under the bed, in a pile on the floor, or knee deep in the closet. Treat them with respect and care—they are valuable accessories that need to be looked after.

✻ Remember that your shoes can make or break an outfit, so always ensure they are in tip-top condition. Steer clear of wearing your "old favorites" if they are scuffed, scratched, or falling to pieces.

Chapter 7

Stockings, Pantyhose, and Underwear

Undergarments are just as important as outer clothes. This is partly because they make you feel confident and sexy, but also because if worn incorrectly they can spoil your silhouette. Every elegant and stylish woman needs to take the time to choose her underwear carefully because it forms the foundation for the finished look. Undergarments are the perfect tools for complementing body shape. They can enhance or support certain areas of the figure, and should be soft and comfortable to wear. Being sophisticated and elegant doesn't mean you can't wear flirty, sexy, and seductive underwear. In fact, these bring out the feminine traits that complete the perfectly dressed woman's image.

———◆———

Panties

That age-old saying "Always wear clean underwear, as you never know what might happen," is very true, but the only reason you should wear clean underwear each day is because it's hygienic. In fact, if you are getting changed for the evening, it's best to change into clean underwear again.

Some women have what they term their "Brigitte Jones knickers"— large, tummy-hugging, comfort panties. These may be acceptable when you are lazing around the house in the knowledge that no one will see them, but when you are out and about, it's better to wear silky French knickers, thongs, women's boxer shorts, or other attractive undergarments.

"I took my knickers off. My friends told me my panty line was visible, so I went without."

Helena Christenson, supermodel

The outer clothes you choose can dictate your choice of lingerie—for example, a figure-hugging dress or skirt demands that you wear a thong, or smooth, invisible or low, hipster panties to avoid a VPL (Visible Panty Line), which spoils the line of your clothes.

The thong is currently the fastest selling style of panties.

Delicate French knickers are flatteringly feminine and perfect under loose-fitting dresses, skirts, and pants. Sexy and alluring, they are comfortable to wear, and they are also ideal for women who are looking for more coverage than a thong can offer.

The female version of the male boxer shorts has become popular. Tighter around the buttocks and on the legs than the men's version, they are the ultimate comfort panties, ideal for wearing under jeans or pantyhose.

The silky La Perla red bra and panties worn by pop star Kylie Minogue on the cover of her 2012 calendar sold for $7,500 (£5,000) at auction in 2011.

The Brassière

Mary Phelps Jacob, an American socialite, was the first woman to patent the brassière as we recognize it today. After purchasing a long, sheer evening gown, Mary realized that wearing the only underwear available at the time—a whale-boned corset—spoiled the line of her dress, as the whale bones were poking out through the sheer fabric. To solve the problem she tied two silk handkerchiefs together with ribbon, creating the first homemade bra, which was the perfect undergarment for the fashions of the time. When they learned of her invention, her friends and family wanted her to make them brassières, so they, too, could wear their dresses in comfort and without restriction. The bra was patented in 1914 as the "backless brassière." It was soft, comfortable, and separated the breasts in a light, natural way.

The word "brassière" is derived from an old French word meaning "upper arm."

Today most women own several bras. Worn for the practicality of supporting the breasts, it has also become one of our greatest fashion accessories. The bra is available in many types ranging from no-nonsense, functional sports bras to luxurious, decadent, lace confections. Some have full cups, others half cups; some are underwired for added support, while others possess extra padding for accentuating the breasts. The bra has evolved dramatically over the decades—now there are even bras that have liquid inside them to create a fuller breast line.

Cleavage (the space between a woman's breasts) is also an important factor in bra design. This area is considered sexy and seductive when exposed, so many modern bras are created to emphasize this aspect of a woman's bust line.

Get yourself measured professionally to find out your correct bra size. Wearing one that is too small is not only uncomfortable, but doesn't give your breasts the right level of support and can ruin your silhouette.

Personally, I find going without a bra unattractive—there is nothing more off-putting than seeing the outline of a woman's nipples through her clothing, although it must be said that some people find this sexy. Going braless is not recommended if you wish to look stylish, so I strongly advise you to wear a bra at all times, especially in public.

All manner of materials are used to enhance the sexiness of bras. Lace and silk are the most traditional embellishments. However, pretty lace creations can show through your clothing, so special T-shirt bras have been designed to be worn under clingy tops and dresses. Lace bras should be reserved for wearing under loose clothing or tops that already feature a textured effect.

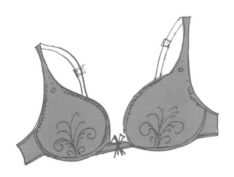

Colors and Prints

Animal prints, bold hues, pastel colors, stripes, spots, and floral prints can all be found decorating both bras and panties and can look impressive, especially when teamed with matching briefs. However, there are a few color match rules when coordinating your underwear with your clothes.

✻ Never wear a black bra under a white top, or black panties under white or pastel colored pants or skirts.

✻ Conversely, avoid wearing a white bra or panties under a sheer dark dress or separates, especially in a nightclub where the fluorescent lights can reveal your white underwear for all to see.

✻ Try to stick to shades close to your natural skin color, or hues that match your clothes unless your outfits are of a thick material—then you can safely leave the house knowing your underwear is not under public scrutiny.

Other more specialized forms of underwear include baby-doll lingerie, chemises, body stockings, and corsets or basques.

Stockings and Pantyhose

Seen as ultra sexy, stockings worn with a garter (suspender) belt have formed part of our underwear since the 1500s when Elizabeth I of England received a pair of knitted silk stockings as a gift. Although the use of hose to protect the legs had been around for much longer, usually in the form of two pieces of leather, woollen or velvet fabric sewn together, it was the pair given to the monarch that set in motion the evolution of stockings down through the centuries into the designs we wear today.

There are, however, downsides to this choice of hosiery. Wearing a garter belt to hold up your stockings under a skirt can be both uncomfortable and fiddly to fasten. In general, women in the twenty-first century tend to wear stockings and garters only when being seductive in the bedroom, or if their mood or place of employment requires an extra bit of sexiness to be added to the outfit.

If you do feel the need to wear stockings, wear them with a skirt that is long enough to cover the stocking tops—revealing thigh flesh is not stylish and looks tasteless. The pencil skirt is the perfect attire for coordinating with stockings.

A more practical alternative to stockings is hold-ups, which still ooze femininity without the encumbrance of the garter belt. However, if the elastic should snap, they could end up wrinkled around your ankles—an embarrassing and definitely unstylish position to find yourself in.

Wearing ordinary stockings or pantyhose with open-toed shoes is a fashion no-no, as it gives your feet a bizarre webbed effect. Only wear them with boots or closed shoes.

Pantyhose (Tights)

Ideally practical for life in the twenty-first century, pantyhose are far more popular today than stockings. They first made an appearance in 1959 in the USA when Glen Raven Mills came up with the inspirational idea of combining panties with hose (stockings). Pantyhose became popular in the '60s when the mini skirt was the height of fashion, and ever since then they have been the most versatile and comfortable hosiery to wear with skirts. Nylon (which was invented in the 1930s) is the most common material used, but pantyhose in other fabrics, such as wool, cotton, and silk, are also available.

The term "denier" relates to the thickness of the yarn from which pantyhose are made. A low denier means the pantyhose are sheerer while a high denier denotes they are thicker.

Varieties of Pantyhose

Thick, opaque pantyhose —These are the best choice for winter, because they are warm and allow you to wear a skirt even in the coldest months. Woollen pantyhose are the thickest of all and will keep your legs protected from the harsh elements. Worn with rubber boots, a short or knee-length jersey dress, and a thick winter coat, they look stylish and cozy; or teamed with a long, oversized sweater and knee-high boots they are casual yet chic.

Thick pantyhose are the perfect winter warmers on a night out and look great worn with a figure-hugging dress and high, platform shoes. Wearing black, opaque pantyhose with a long-sleeved T-shirt under a sleeveless lightweight dress, teamed with a pair of knee-length boots, is a great way to enjoy your summer clothes all year round.

Sexy, sheer, nylons—These can be worn by all women and are suitable for almost all occasions. Ideal for the summer, ultra-sheer, almost transparent pantyhose give the illusion of being bare legged. Pantyhose in natural skin tones also complement a summer tea dress when worn with pumps for a casual daytime look. A sheer pair of black, navy, or flesh-colored pantyhose worn with a business suit portrays an instant air of professionalism. Sheer pantyhose can be worn with any skirt or evening dress to add the finishing touch of sophistication to the outfit.

Motifs—Recent fashions have sparked off a renewed interest in pantyhose featuring motifs. Embellished in many different ways, such as stars, flowers, sparkles, spots, or stripes, you can even buy pantyhose that resemble stockings and garter belts—so you can have the sexy, flirtatious look without the discomfort of having to wear a lacy belt.

Jazz up your style by wearing colored pantyhose that coordinate with your outfits.

Chapter 8

Accessories

*"I adore wearing gems, but not because
they are mine. You can't possess radiance,
you can only admire it."*
Elizabeth Taylor, actress and style icon

Accessorize, accessorizes, accessorize! Precious
gems, such as diamonds, rubies, emeralds, and
sapphires, set in gold, silver, or platinum always
dazzle. But high-quality costume jewelry can be
equally striking when worn with confidence.
Choosing the perfect jewels is crucial for completing
your look, especially if you are endeavoring to
display a total image of sophisticated elegance.
Necklaces, earrings, bracelets, and rings are able to
enhance your image, add depth to an outfit, and
reveal your inner class—but only if worn in a tasteful
and chic manner.

———◆———

For millennia both men and women have adorned themselves with
decorative jewelry. In most cases it was to demonstrate their status,

sometimes to ward off evil spirits, but more often to tie in with fashion trends and enhance the beauty of the wearer.

Nothing much has changed—except maybe wearing jewels to keep evil spirits at bay isn't quite as popular now!) However, we are still seduced by pretty, sparkling jewelry today and status can still be displayed through jewels. The more financially affluent women, or, of course, those who have wealthy partners, are able to afford fine jewelry that is historically valuable or made by well-known designers. But while some of us may own one or two valuable pieces, the rest of our jewelry is of the costume variety.

The term "costume jewelry" refers to adornments made from non-precious metals created from faux pearls, imitation stones, and manmade crystals, which are set in base metal rather than gold, silver, or platinum. This form of decorative jewelry became popular in the twentieth century, and in most cases the jewelry is just as beautifully crafted as fine pieces and often can be valuable as well as stylish.

In fact, costume jewelry is the most usual type of accessory worn by women today. You can purchase matching sets, statement pieces, or dainty, demure items that make as much impact as precious pieces that cost a fortune.

The all-important style statement comes with how you wear your jewelry. Avoid looking like Mr T from the A-Team with many strands of gold necklaces or wearing rings on every finger—this is just not tasteful. Your jewelry should complement your clothes by creating an impression of fluidity in your overall look.

Demure But Dynamic Daytime

At times you need to wear understated accessories, especially for a business meeting or on a day out with the family. A pretty pendant on a silver or gold chain, some beads, or a string of pearls are all perfect for such occasions.

Pearls

Classic pearls, whether imitation or cultured, deliver a simple, pure effect and are ideal for wearing with a pant or skirt suit for work engagements. You can then add a pair of single-pearl, drop earrings and a brooch to marry the accessories together. This was a favorite combination of Coco Chanel, who wore pearls by the yard, often in multiple strands.

Wearing jangling earrings, necklaces, or bracelets when trying to deliver a business pitch to clients can take the focus away from your ideas and onto your jewelry, so keep your adornments low-key in the work environment.

Beads

The Summer of Love of 1967 has been superseded by the Summer of Festivals but maxi dresses are still the most popular attire. For that authentic '60s and '70s "flower-power" look, add a tribal-inspired necklace or a long string of wooden beads to replicate this era. Beaded bracelets and, if you dare, a beaded ankle bracelet will also evoke a hippie style. Plastic, wooden, and glass beads in a whole range of colors actually works really well with most daytime outfits, too.

Worn with plain tops or shift dresses, they look great when you coordinate the colors. For a more striking effect wear vibrant beads against a more neutral backdrop.

Enamel

One of the classiest styles of jewelry, enamel work is enjoying renewed popularity. During the Art Nouveau movement of the late nineteenth and early twentieth centuries enamel decoration was often found on pendants and brooches. Work by designers such as Charles Horner and Archibald Knox was among the most sought after. Today, enameled pendants, earrings, bracelets, and rings are very popular, especially with those who have sophisticated tastes. Simple and stylish, these pieces are often dainty and so can be worn with any daytime outfit, or teamed with a simple evening dress for a dinner date.

Gold and Silver Necklaces

Many women own a gold or silver necklace that has a sentimental value because it is a treasured gift or was inherited from a family member or dear friend. Lockets and pendants are popular examples, while plain chains appeal to some women. The most common of all jewelry, this type of adornment is generally worn on a daily basis. The wearer often takes it off only when she wants to wear something a little more extravagant.

Making a Statement

There was a time when big, bold necklaces that made a statement were reserved for the evening, but over the decades this has changed and now women sport large, ostentatious necklaces and equally show-stopping rings throughout the day.

Available in a wealth of different materials, modern jewelry can be made from resin, plastic, stainless steel, and even fabric. Other materials used include mother-of-pearl, shells, wood, and copper. Designs and styles vary from naturalistic subjects, such as flowers and animals, to stylized abstract forms and meaningful symbols. There is literally a piece to suit every woman's taste and pocket, as well as something that works well with each and every form of clothing.

"Jewelry takes people's minds off your wrinkles."
Sonja Henie, figure skater and film star

Lavish, Opulent Evenings

Diamonds are, of course, the favorite with the majority of women and if you are fortunate enough to own a few, you will surely want to show them off. Although actress and keen collector of jewelry the late Elizabeth Taylor once said, "Big girls need big diamonds," many of us are not in the position to acquire opulent jewels. Instead we wear costume jewelry, which can often have a similar effect, especially if we opt for something vintage, such as diamanté.

Cruising the High Seas

An invitation to dine at the Captain's table on board a cruise liner demands exquisite dress. So to highlight your stunning floor-length evening gown, wear a showy, sparkling necklace, matching drop earrings, a glitzy bracelet, and a large dress ring. Obviously, this is the perfect occasion for precious jewels if you have them, but if you haven't, you can still dazzle with vintage Austrian crystals or alternatively invest in contemporary crystal pieces created by Swarovski, Butler and Wilson, or another modern maker.

The Black-tie Event

Sparkling jewels again are ideal for that extra special evening dinner or ball. Even if your dress glitters and sparkles, you can still wear extra bling in the form of accessories, but perhaps tie them in with the dominant color of your dress to make them more subtle, and be careful not to overdo the look.

Dinner with Friends

Anything goes, depending on which outfit you choose. If you go for a more casual look, coordinate it with beads, silver, or an attractive necklace that makes a statement. If the look you have opted for is slightly more dressy, you can introduce some sparkle but not as much as you would wear to a more formal evening.

Rings

Big bulky rings have become all the rage of late. Available in many designs created from all types of material, they work well for both day and evening wear. Rings bring attention to your hands so ensure you have manicured nails when you wear them—bitten, dirty, or stubby nails are most off-putting.

Always wear your dress rings on the right hand, as your left should be reserved for your engagement, eternity, and wedding rings.

Iconic Famous Jewels

Wallis Simpson's onyx and diamond panther bracelet, created for Cartier by the jeweller Jeanne Toussaint in 1952, sold for $6.78m (£4.52m), while her ruby, sapphire, emerald, citrine, and diamond brooch clip in the form of a flamingo sold for $2.58m (£1.72m) at Sotheby's auction house in London in 2010.

The ring presented to Jacqueline Kennedy by Aristotle Onassis when she accepted his marriage proposal is one of the most famous modern rings. Believed to have been worn only twice by Jacqueline Kennedy Onassis, it comprises the Lesotho III 40-carat marquise diamond and it sold for $2.6m (£1.75m) in 1996.

The late Elizabeth Taylor's jewelry was put up for sale at Christie's in 2011 and made a grand total of $112.5m (£74.9m.) Among her extraordinary jewels was "La Peregrina" (meaning pilgrim or wanderer), a magnificent pearl set in a Cartier ruby and diamond necklace. This sixteenth-century pearl was bought at auction for Taylor by her husband, Richard Burton, in 1969 as a Valentine's gift. It cost $37,000 (£25,500.) Once owned by Mary Tudor and having been depicted in famous artworks over the centuries, La Peregrina is one of the most notorious pearls of all time. You can imagine the panic when Taylor lost it, only to find it being chewed upon by one of her puppies. Thankfully she managed to retrieve the precious pearl, which luckily hadn't suffered any damage. When this necklace came up for sale after Taylor's death, it sold for a record-breaking $11.4m (£7.6m.)

Caring for Your Jewelry

✱ Keep your precious jewels in their original case or neatly in a jewelry box, so that necklaces do not tangle or get knotted, earrings are not lost and, more importantly, you know where every item is when you are ready to wear it.

✱ Ensure your precious gems and metals are clean. You can wash jewelry by dipping it in warm soapy water, gently cleaning the stones in silver and gold mounts with an old toothbrush. Then rinse the pieces and pat them dry with a soft cloth.

✱ Remove jewelry when you come into contact with chemicals. So no jumping into the hot tub wearing valuable jewels, as the chloride and bromide can damage metals and stones! The same applies to swimming pools.

✱ Try not to knock your rings, because soft stones, such as onyx, can crack easily.

Purses (Handbags) and Bags

It is a well-known fact that all women love purses. Many of us own far more than we actually need. Originating in prehistoric times for practical uses, such as carrying food and flints, these humble receptacles have evolved over the millennia to become one of our favorite status symbols when it comes to stylish accessories.

The secret to carrying a great purse with style lies in knowing which shape best suits the occasion. It is therefore advisable to own purses in a variety of shapes to cover every eventuality. Also ensure you buy purses in a range of colors to match your outfits. For example, autumnal colors are perfect for business occasions, while vibrant chintz floral patterns and pastel hues are ideal for the purses and bags you'll use in the summer months.

The Classic Purse

Available in various shapes and sizes, this purse can be carried by its short handle and usually has a longer strap inside so that it can be worn over the shoulder, too. Produced in every color imaginable, the classic purse is good for both day and evening. One of the most famous is the "Kelly Bag," which was first introduced by the French fashion house Hermès in 1935. Completely handmade, a genuine Hermès Kelly can sell for thousands of dollars—that's if you are lucky enough to get hold of one! It can take years, sometimes even a lifetime, to acquire this most sought-after bag, as the waiting list is so long. However, all is not lost as there are many other purses similar to the "Kelly Bag" out there at much more affordable prices.

The Shoulder Purse

This appealing yet practical type of purse is hugely popular with women who work in offices or are on the move constantly during the day. It is wise to own one in a neutral color, so that it goes well with any outfit of any color and so can be used daily.

The Vintage Box Purse

In the 1950s, hard Lucite box bags become fashionable in America. These vintage pieces are now highly prized by women looking for a quirkier than usual daytime bag. Sensational to look at, these bags are very heavy to carry and do not hold much in the way of personal items, so it's best to limit their use to when you want to make a big impression at a special event.

Coordinate the bag you carry with your jewelry as well as your clothes and shoes to give a bolder statement to your style.

The Clutch Purse

This purse is visually very elegant, making it the perfect evening bag, especially if covered in sequins, sparkles, or faux gems. They come in all materials, colors, and some innovative styles.

The Tote Bag

A stylish tote bag is ideal for daytime, especially if you are a mom, as it is big enough to hold all those essential items that you need every time you leave the house with your child. Tote means to carry and the term is used to describe a diversity of styles—these bags can be upright or squat, handles long or short, and they come in either natural or synthetic material.

The Basket Weave

A very popular summer bag, the basket weave is the ultimate accessory if you are going on a picnic or out walking in the meadows during hot, hazy days. They can be folksy, retro, funky or understated, depending on the image you want to convey.

Chapter 9

Vintage Fashion

We owe so much to the fashions of the past.
There is no doubt that we wouldn't have the style-
packed wardrobes that we have today if it wasn't for
the influential designers and their innovative
clothing creations of times gone by. A huge influence
on contemporary clothes, vintage fashions have
inspired many of the looks that we wear on a daily
basis. But rather than replicating past times
with contemporary takes, why not invest in
a few genuine vintage pieces to add originality
to your own unique style.

Wearing vintage clothes has become bang on trend of late with all age groups desperate to acquire pieces evocative of their favorite bygone eras. The most desirable examples can now command huge amounts of money, especially as A-list celebrities, museums, and vintage clothes stores are all vying to obtain those exquisite garments. Sadly, a 1920s Chanel LBD or a 1970s Ossie Clarke/Celia Birtwell maxi dress is nowadays accessible only for those who have deep pockets, but it's still possible to hunt out affordable pieces that have just as much elegance and style without the eye-watering price tag. A great way to add interest to your wardrobe staples is to mix and match vintage with modern. This is not difficult to do and will upgrade and enhance your current look.

Evocative of an Era

To carry off the look successfully, it is crucial to choose the era that will work best with your personality, body shape, age, and style. You may well be a "child of the '60s," but that doesn't mean that over fifty years on you will still look fabulous in a mini dress that used to turn heads—in fact, the probability is that you definitely won't! So forget the clothes you used to wear back in the good old days, and concentrate on hunting out vintage pieces that will suit you now.

The Roaring '20s

In the 1920s, fashions changed dramatically with the raising of hemlines and liberation from corsets, and it remains a popular era when it comes to acquiring vintage clothes. The flapper-girl dresses of the '20s are still very much in vogue, with modern replicas hitting the stores every season. Comprising fringe tiers, sheer bodices, and tasteful embellishments, these dresses were shin- or knee-length and generally sleeveless. Other notable clothing styles of this period include knitwear featuring geometric patterns, Egyptian-inspired designs due to the discovery of Tutankhamun's tomb by Howard Carter in 1922, and exotic, Oriental-influenced silk kimonos, dresses, and evening coats.

Wear it now—A young, flirtatious style, the 1920s flapper-girl look suits only women with a boyish figure, as it was created for the less curvy, slimmer body shape. A vintage fringed or drop-waisted flapper dress will always remain an evening staple—its simple shift style has timeless appeal. Complete the authentic look by wearing a long string of beads and a pair of Mary-Jane shoes. Wrist bags were all the rage in the '20s, so carry one of these for your lipstick.

The Golden '30s

The Golden Age of Hollywood led the way during the 1930s by introducing sleek, feminine elegance into the fashion scene. Tailored work wear, afternoon tea dresses, women's pants, flowing evening dresses with touches of Victorian influence and worn with fur capes, stoles, and coats—these are the fashions that dominated the decade.

Wear it now—Voluptuous ladies with feminine curves are well equipped to carry off the sexy styles of the 1930s, as this era celebrated the woman with a fuller figure. Wide-legged pants worn with halter-neck tops may not become your wardrobe staples, nor will the touches of Victorian styling, but if you are seeking a true, vintage-'30s ensemble to complement your figure, opt for tailored work wear, which has remained, and will continue to be, a classic style. For example, wearing a tweed skirt that falls straight from the waist to the calf and is fitted tightly on the waist line but flares out over the hips will ensure you are one of the most smartly dressed women in the office. Wear a soft blouse or a smart shirt with it, and brown, two-tone pumps with rounded toes to complete a look that was the height of fashion in the '30s.

The Wartime '40s

Due to the outbreak of World War II, fashionable women in this decade were not concerned with new fashion trends, but rather adopted the attitude of "making do and mending" the clothes they already had. Military styles became fashionable with jackets sporting wide-cut, padded shoulders. The first-ever jumpsuit, known as the Siren Suit, was perfect for throwing on when dashing to the air-raid shelter, while evening wear consisted largely of simple dresses that women created themselves from fabrics found around the home. Floral prints were ubiquitous, as women tried to turn their backs on the austere times by infusing color into their evening wardrobe. The 1940s tea dress is another item that would have been adapted from a dress the woman already owned or home-made from curtains or bedspread fabric.

Wear it now—You can still source floral dresses from the 1940s in vintage stores and at fairs for very reasonable prices and as they come in a host of styles there is something to suit every age and body shape. The ideal summer garment for any activity, wear your floral dress with bare legs and a pair of court shoes. If you are attending one of the many themed 1940s events held all year round, really go to town with the whole '40s look by adding a pair of gloves, clip-on earrings, and a string of pearls, and perching a small hat on your head. It's likely that the dress alone will gain staple status in your wardrobe, but you will have great fun joining in the '40's frolics dressed head to toe in the vintage style.

Condition is paramount in vintage pieces—only ever buy them if they are in mint condition—and always check the whole garment for tears, water and sweat stains, and botched alterations.

The Fabulous '50s

The 1950s were an elegant decade when women presented themselves in a "lady-like" manner by dressing in feminine, structured clothes. The pencil and circle skirts, tailored suits worn with wrist gloves, matching shoes and purses, as well as Capri pants, shirtwaister dresses, and knitwear were the items worn most often. For evening, there were two looks: elegant cocktail dresses or extravagant ball gowns. This was also the decade when the teenager was born, and fashion sub-cultures sprang up, such as the Beatniks, who wore tight-fitting pants with black turtle-neck sweaters, and the Teddy girls or rockabillies, who teamed pencil or petticoat skirts with mohair jumpers or low-cut tops. They wore their hair in quiffed ponytails and would never contemplate leaving the house without first applying bright red lipstick.

Wear it now—Rather than dressing in the usual '50s circle skirt or tailored suit, try replicating style-icon Grace Kelly's look with a pair of snug-fitting Capri pants. Team them with a boat-necked peplum top or a knitted roll-neck, and add a neck-tie scarf and sling-back court shoes to accessorize. This casual yet smart outfit is fabulous for wearing to a summer barbecue or a day out at a vintage car show.

The Swinging '60s

New trends constantly emerge throughout the 1960s, and this is probably the most exciting decade in the twentieth century for fashion. Haute couture virtually disappeared to be replaced by ready-to-wear street styles. The Mod look created by designer Mary Quant dominated the early to mid-60s, her most famous creation being the mini skirt. The A-line skirt or dress was also prolific, along with the Empire-line "baby-doll," a style in which the dress is gathered under the bust.

Boutiques replaced clothes stores, one of the most famous being the legendary Biba in London, which was established by Barbara Hulanicki in 1964. Styles from the Victorian, Edwardian, Art Nouveau, and Art Deco periods were the main inspirations for Biba's fashion lines, which often incorporated appliqué work and lace.

In past decades women were generally much smaller than they are today, so always try on vintage clothes before you buy them. This also applies to sizing, which was not as generous as it is today, so you might find that you need to trade up a size or more in both clothes and footwear.

In the 1960s designers experimented with patterns and materials. Fabrics featuring Op-art (optical illusions) became widespread as did psychedelic, swirling colors. Vibrant hues in lime green, orange, and yellow were popular with the younger generations. Even material didn't escape this revolutionary period in fashion—you could wear anything from a dress made from chain mail to a disposable paper garment advertising a famous soup brand.

Wear it now—The 1960s were perhaps the most fun time for fashion and there is only one vintage staple you need to incorporate from this decade into your wardrobe and that's the mini dress. Reserved for women with a slim figure and, of course, amazing legs, the mini should have that '60s flair but also be classic enough to be worn time and time again. Find a summer version in swirling pastel shades, or for a winter mini choose a shift style in a vibrant color to wear with pantyhose and knee-high "go-go" boots. If you can afford to, think about investing in a piece by a named designer, such as Mary Quant or Foale & Tuffin, for extra kudos.

The Hippie '70s

Fashion was confused during the 1970s, as there was such an eclectic mixture of styles to choose from. Some of the dominant types of clothing included ethnic-inspired embroidered kaftans, waistcoats, floral cotton skirts and dresses, vibrantly colored "loons" (wide bell-bottomed pants,) smocks, spandex tube tops, and lycra pants, as well as fluorescent satin dresses, the glittery gold lamé of glam rock, and the bondage pants popularized by the new sub-culture of punk.

Wear it now—Depending on your fashion tastes, the '70s had much to offer—but not necessarily as a total look. The obvious choice, which is still very much of the moment, is the ethnic maxi dress, but you could always take odd pieces from the '70s trends and team them with your modern classics. In the 1970s knitwear was a big story and was popular in every style, from big, chunky cardigans to knitted tanktops. British designer Bill Gibb was renowned for his knitted outfits, which today can command hundreds of dollars. To get the authentic '70s look, try teaming a tank top with a long-sleeved shirt, a pair of pants with a slight flare, and a floppy felt hat. This is a style that can be carried off elegantly in the twenty-first century, and if you are feeling very brave, add a vintage pair of platform shoes.

The Yuppie '80s

Steer clear of buying into this decade. In my opinion, there was absolutely nothing stylish about the 1980s. Ra-ra and puff-ball skirts, padded "power" shoulders, and clothing emblazoned with logos are just not the way forward for the seriously elegant woman. A disastrous fashion decade—I would avoid it like the plague!

Combining Vintage with Contemporary

Garments that subtly allude to vintage style can be worn at any time, so don't feel you have to dress head-to-toe in fashions from a particular era. Pick key pieces and merge them with contemporary classics for a fantastic, dramatic effect. Being stylish is all about individuality, so by mixing genuine vintage clothing and accessories with your usual modern clothes, you will always have a unique outfit.

Chapter 10

Casual, Informal, and Formal Wear

**In order to achieve the status of being a style icon
you need to have a fully stocked wardrobe and be
prepared for every social eventuality. The elegant
and sophisticated woman is always aware of how to
dress appropriately, whether she is out shopping
with friends or invited onboard a yacht; she
understands fashion etiquette when attending a
wedding and how to shine when walking along the
red carpet. Projecting star style-quality at all times,
she is a woman who knows how to dress for the
occasion, exuding panache wherever she goes.**

———◆———

Casual Wear

Don't be tempted to throw on the first clothes that come to hand,
even if you are just popping out to the store for some milk. You need
to dress to perfection at all times and that includes when dressing
casually. Imagine if you bumped into an old boy- or girlfriend (which
is possible) and you looked anything but sensational—this could be
embarrassing. Even spontaneously hooking up with friends when you

are looking unkempt and scruffy wouldn't make you feel great about yourself, so always be aware that any situation could arise when you go through your door, and be prepared.

The trick is to organize your clothes the night before, think carefully about what you might be doing, and consider which outfit best suits the occasion. This not only will ensure you have your style in place, but also saves you rushing around in the morning frantically looking for garments that are still sitting in the washing basket.

Wearing casual attire isn't an excuse for sloppy dressing—in fact, it can be extremely stylish. A term coined by many is "smart casual," which is a perfect way to describe your daytime ensemble. If you get into the habit of always wearing chic clothes no matter what your day holds, you are well on your way to becoming an immaculately dressed woman.

Jeans

Denim jeans have come a long way since their introduction as work clothes for laborers and slaves during the eighteenth century. In fact, rare vintage Levi's are highly sought after by collectors, who are willing to pay a premium to own them. Today, jeans are the uniform of the masses and, as they are available in a range of cuts, styles, and price brackets, they are the most common casual garments found in our wardrobe. If worn correctly, they can look elegant and stylish, but if worn incorrectly, they project a scruffy, untidy image, so it is important to know your jeans and how to wear them.

Straight Cut

With the shape and size of the legs remaining consistent from the thighs to the ankles, these jeans sit naturally on the waist. They are ideal for all body shapes and are the smartest of the jean family because they resemble straight-cut pants.

The oldest known pair of Levi 501 jeans, dating back to the 1880s, were discovered in a disused Colorado mine. The Levi company paid more than $46,500 (£31,000) to buy them back so that they could put them in their museum.

Skinny

Tight and figure-hugging, these jeans look fabulous if you have a slim figure, especially if you have small buttocks and long legs.

Boyfriend

Low-rise baggy jeans, these slouch from the hip down the legs, so it looks as if you are wearing a pair of men's jeans (hence the name "boyfriend") even though they are specifically cut for a woman's body shape. Popular among the younger generations, these jeans fit the majority of body shapes.

Flares

These jeans fit tightly over the hips and are tapered down the thigh, flaring out from the knee to the ankle. They are not as wide as 1970s bell bottoms, but still have a noticeable A-line shape from the knee downward.

Boot Leg (Boot Cut)

So called because you can wear boots underneath them without the jeans crinkling up, these jeans are tapered down to the knee and then become looser over the calves to give more room at the ankle. Again, this style of jeans suits most body shapes.

All jeans are ideal for casual daytime activities. During the winter months they are comfortable and cozy to slip on, while in the summer you can opt for cropped, three-quarter length jeans or denim shorts (or even a denim skirt.) Jeans also now come in a variety of colors other than the traditional dark and light blues, with black and white being the most popular. Don't be afraid to wear brightly colored jeans either. Red, green, purple, and orange can all look great when worn with coordinating tops, especially in the summer.

Casual Style Guide

So what should you wear when you need to look casual but at the same time portray an image of elegant chic?

The School Run

Many moms are inclined to dress in joggers and Ugg boots to take their children to school. Even though this is a quick and comfortable option, there is no need to dress scruffily, especially if you want to make a good impression on the teachers and other moms at the school gate. A floral tea dress or maxi worn with wedge sandals and a denim jacket is pretty for the summer and easy to wear. In winter go for boot-leg jeans teamed with a vibrantly colored sweater. Color lifts your spirits so you will particularly benefit from this when you have to leave the house in inclement weather.

"I wish I had invented blue jeans. They have expression, modesty, sex appeal, simplicity. All I hope for in my clothes."

Yves Saint Laurent, fashion designer

Meeting for Lunch

More or less anything goes as long as it looks smart and stylish: a short dress worn with opaque pantyhose and boots; a pair of jeans with the staple white shirt or smock blouse; cropped pants in pastel hues with a T-shirt. These are all casual enough to wear for a lunch date, but will still portray a chic and fashionable image.

Girl about Town

When out participating in what is probably the favorite pastime of females—shopping—you want to feel as comfortable as you can. Bear in mind that you may be walking around for hours, and wear clothes that are easy to slip on and off, as you will probably try on a few new outfits. An ensemble that fits the bill is a pair of skinny jeans in any color, worn with a long, figure-hugging T-shirt (no buttons to undo) that reaches below the crotch, and either a smart blazer or, if it's a hot summer's day, a waistcoat, for a touch of added panache. Flat knee-high boots or ballet pumps should be your footwear of choice—you don't want to have to abandon your shopping expedition because your feet are hurting.

The Cinema Date

Just because you are sitting down in a dark auditorium doesn't mean you need to pay less attention to your clothing. Again, comfort is paramount, as you will be sitting down for a few hours—a jersey wool dress is ideal, or baggy, straight-cut jeans teamed with a long-sleeved sweater and ankle boots. These will allow you to relax and give your full attention to the film.

Picnic in the Park

For this type of summer event a floral wrap dress or a 1950s-style wide skirt or dress worn with decorative sandals will keep you feeling cool and looking elegant while you eat strawberries and drink champagne from your wicker picnic basket. A sun hat and cardigan will also come in useful in case the weather turns chilly.

The trick to choosing any casual outfit is to assess the situation beforehand. Comfort is imperative no matter what type of activity you will be taking part in, and you might also want to impress the person or people you are with. All it needs is a little thought and effort to accomplish your desired look.

Informal Outfits

Always a gray area, dressing informally can be daunting because you really need to get your outfit just right, otherwise you could spend your whole time at the event feeling uncomfortable or, in the worst case scenario, you could even be turned away. Slightly more dressy than casual, but not as demanding as formal, it's a look that really does need some pre-planning.

Ladies' Day at the Races

Going to the races is a prime example of a well-known informal occasion when your outfit needs to have extra flair and flamboyance. An eye-catching dress that comes to just below or on the knee is ideal, and color is a must—the brighter the better. Stick to one strong color or go for a floral pattern—either will look good. Wear a loose-fitting garment for comfort, as it can be a long day, and take a risk by wearing an extravagant hat. You should also wear heels to accentuate your femininity and, of course, take an evening-style matching purse in which to hold all your essentials, including all the cash you will receive from your winnings!

The Wedding

A wedding is the bride's big day, so please don't treat it as an opportunity to showcase your most extravagant outfit and accessories. Understated elegance is what you need to project when you attend a wedding, and etiquette dictates that you must never wear white, cream, or ivory. Any other color is acceptable, depending on the season, although pastels are the most appropriate shades and should be worn in the form of dresses, skirts, and complementary blouses or tops, or suits, which are also popular wedding attire for guests.

The Christening

A true fashionista always wants to look her best, so even if you have not been asked to be a god-parent, a christening is still a another great opportunity to get dressed up. A good choice for this occasion would be a skirt or pants suit in a pastel hue, worn with a soft, pussy-bow blouse in a contrasting color, and kitten heels. This is an ideal outfit for a summer event. For winter, look stylish wearing a shirt dress with a bolero and knee-length boots.

The Funeral

As a mark of respect, black is the only color you should wear at a funeral, as we have already mentioned (see page 18), but that doesn't mean you cannot adopt a sophisticated informal style for your outfit. The LBD is the most common choice, but a smart skirt or a pant suit, or even an elegant wrap dress are all suitable attire.

A Cocktail Party

A cocktail dress is the obvious choice to wear to a cocktail party. It should be knee length and have a full skirt, although a more restrictive tighter shape is also acceptable. You should wear it with killer heels, sparkling accessories, and a shimmering bolero. Sartorial elegance is a must for these occasions.

A Night at the Theatre

Long gone are the days when women wore floor-length formal evening gowns and men black-tie suits when visiting the theatre or opera. With less restrictive dress codes the majority of people now dress smartly but informally (although there are some who think it's acceptable to dress casually.) Smart pants worn with flowing tops are a comfortable option, with some sparkle either on the top or in the form of jewelry adding that extra-special flair.

Formal Attire

There is little call for formal wear in today's society, so many women never get to experience the joy of feeling like a real princess in a floor-length gown and glittering jewelry. This is a shame as it's one of the most feminine and striking ensembles, and can make a woman feel like a million dollars.

On a Cruise

Official dinners on board cruise ships afford the perfect excuse to dress in full formal regalia. There are always two or three evenings when sweeping, floor-length gowns are required by the strict dress code. There is nothing more glamorous than walking along the deck of an ocean liner with your dress skimming the ground. It's as if you've been transported back in time to the 1920s and the golden age of travel—a really magical experience. Any color gown is acceptable, but black is always the most elegant and striking. However, for a more fun option choose vibrant jewel-like colors so you stand out. The glitzier the jewelry the better, and a faux fur stole across the shoulders adds instant elegance.

On the Red Carpet

If you are fortunate enough to be invited to a film première or other event where you need to walk on the red carpet, wearing a long gown will always attract positive attention. Backless, low-cut, vintage, and modern styles are all suitable. One of the best options is to wear something unique, which is still classically cut—that way you won't end up on the "worst dressed" list! Always team your dress with understated jewels for a "less-is-more" effect, and high heels.

However, as your shoes will be hidden under the gown, you could get away with lower kitten heels if you find high heels very uncomfortable.

The Black-tie Event

This is another occasion when you must adhere to a strict dress code, as women are required to wear formal long gowns to complement the men in their tuxedos and dress shirts. Once again there isn't much to add because when you wear a floor-length evening dress you exude femininity, elegance, and sophistication.

Very few women get it wrong when they have to wear formal dress, as the gowns speak for themselves. The only spin you can put on your outfit is to pick a dress that reflects your own personality by choosing colors that complement your skin tone and a design that accentuates your body shape.

Chapter 11

The Good Grooming Guide

It is all well and good mastering the art of dressing
to impress, but if you fail to maintain a polished
appearance in all areas, it can spoil your total look.
Being immaculately groomed is essential because
putting clothes on an unwashed body, having lank
and greasy hair, or smelling of stale body odor
is completely off-putting to those around you and is
totally unacceptable in today's society. You need
to shine from head to toe by smelling delightful
and looking fabulous in order to achieve
the coveted status of being a completely chic
and stylish woman.

———◆———

Cleanliness

I cannot stress enough how important it is to wash and shower regularly.

✱ For that extra relaxing treat, run a bubble bath, light some candles, and enjoy your bathing experience.

✱ Use soap, shower gel, and occasionally a body scrub.

✱ Wash your hands regularly throughout the day, especially after visiting the bathroom.

Skin

A healthy, glowing skin is the foundation of every woman's beauty.

✱ Cleanse, tone, and moisturize your face and neck every morning and evening.

✱ Use a body scrub at least once a week and apply body butter or moisturizer every day after a shower.

✱ If your pocket allows, treat yourself to a professional facial and a full body massage once a month to keep your skin healthy and release tension from your muscles.

✱ Get enough sleep—if you don't, your skin will look tired and dark bags will appear under your eyes.

✱ Drink plenty of water during the day, as it hydrates the body and keeps your skin supple and youthful.

✱ Invest in an expensive tinted moisturizer for that quick, daytime fix.

Hair

Your hair is your crowning glory, so it needs always to look sleek and shiny.

✱ Wash and condition your hair at least every other day and make regular trips to the hairdresser for that all-important trim.

✱ If you color your hair, never let your roots grow out too far before retouching.

✱ Always keep a brush or comb in your purse, as windswept hair is just not a stylish look.

Nails

Hands are an important focal point, especially if you gesticulate with them when you speak, so ensure that you keep your nails free from dirt and well manicured.

✱ If you wear varnish, make sure that you look after it—chipped varnish can instantly ruin your whole look.

✱ The same applies to toe nails. No-one likes to see unpainted, uncared for toes peeping out from your sandals. It is paramount, especially in the summer, to have a professional pedicure at least once a month.

✱ Apply hand cream every day to keep your hands soft and supple.

Waxing

Hairy legs are a definite turn-off and do not look attractive when you wear a short dress or skirt, so it's important to keep your legs hair-free.

✱ Although shaving does remove the majority of hair, it's better to have a professional wax. This will ensure your legs stay silky smooth for much longer.

✱ Other visible areas should also be free from hair, the most important being just above your upper lip—wax it off!

✱ Never over-pluck your eyebrows—always keep their natural line.

Make-up

To look glamorous and stylish, you should ensure that your make-up always complements your look.

* Whenever possible use subtle, natural shades, which are far more flattering than wearing too much heavy make-up. Looking as if you plastered on your foundation, lipstick, and blusher with a trowel is not attractive and certainly not stylish.

* The eyes are said to be the "windows to the soul" and are one of a woman's most attractive features. A touch of mascara and eye liner can really open up your eye area, so even if you don't have time to do your whole face, always try and make-up your eyes.

* Wear colors that suit your skin tone. If you are unsure, speak to a consultant at the beauty counter in your local department store for advice on which shades to choose.

* Always remove your make-up before going to bed at night.

Fragrance

As well as looking great, a stylish woman must also smell lovely.

* Perfume is a very personal choice, especially as one brand can smell completely different on one woman from the way it smells on another. Always try a sample before buying a perfume, and wear it for 10–15 minutes before deciding if it smells good on you.

* Wear a light floral scent throughout the day and a heavier fragrance for the evening.

* Always apply perfume to your pulse points on your wrists, behind your knees, and at the back of your ears—these send out the scent.

* Don't rub your wrists together after applying your perfume—this lessens the smell.

* Buy and wear body lotion in the same scent as your perfume, because this will make your perfume's fragrance last longer.

* Ensure you are not wearing an overpowering amount of perfume —spray it on in short bursts rather than long blasts.

* It is proven that perfume can have a dramatic effect on improving your mood, so try to wear your favorite scent every day.

The Breath

No stylish woman can afford to have bad breath. Reasons for this affliction include drinking too many cups of coffee and eating particularly strong or pungent food.

* To avoid bad breath, pay attention to your dental hygiene by cleaning your teeth regularly.

* Floss between your teeth daily.

* Use mouthwash after you have brushed your teeth.

* Spray your mouth with a breath freshener after eating.

And finally...

Ensure you keep every essential beauty product, breath freshener, make-up, perfume, and your hair brush in your stylish purse, so that you can freshen up whenever the need arises.

Being a style icon demands a great deal of attention to detail and it is only when you have perfected your dress style, coordinated your accessories, and polished your appearance that you can proudly announce to the world that you are now a beautifully dressed and immaculately groomed woman, who recognizes the importance of style.

Index